101
SPLIT 4-4 STUNTS

LEO HAND

©2003 Coaches Choice. All rights reserved. Printed in the United States.

No part of this book may be reproduced, stored in a retrieval system or transmitted in any form or by any means, electronic, mechanical, photocopying, recording or otherwise, without the written permission of Coaches Choice.

ISBN: 1-58518-707-0
Library of Congress Control Number: 2002109167
Cover design: Kerry Hartjen
Diagrams and Layout: Deborah Oldenburg
Front cover photo: Tom Hauck/Allsport

Coaches Choice
PO Box 1828
Monterey, CA 93942
www.coacheschoice.com

DEDICATION

FOR MARY

AND OUR NINE CHILDREN:
MARY, PHILOMENA, JIHAN, RAINA, MICHAEL,
DAVID, KAHLIL, ERNIE, AND RUDY

AND OUR PARENTS:
DOROTHY HAND, JULIA YAZZIE, LEO HAND,
AND DON KEE YAZZIE.

ACKNOWLEDGMENTS

Thanks to Tony Shaw for giving me the opportunity to coach in Texas.

Thanks to Jim Murphy, Don Kloppenberg, and Will Shaw for all they taught me about defense at Long Beach City College.

Thanks to the wonderful people of the Zuni and Navajo Nations who taught me much more than I taught them during the seven years I lived with them.

Thanks to Joe Griffin for giving me one of the best coaching jobs in California.

Thanks to all of the splendid young men whom I have been privileged to coach.

Thanks to all of the great coaches whom I have been fortunate to have worked with and coached against.

Thanks to Phil Johnson for all of his help and kind words.

Thanks to Conrado Ronquillo, Joe Barba, and the maintenance crew at Irvin High School for all of their patience, kindness, and help during this project.

Thanks to Sam Snoddy for his assistance during this project.

Thanks to the offspring of the ancestors who endured the *Middle Chamber* and the *Long Walk* for all of the contributions that they have made to the greatest game of all.

Thanks to Howard Wells for giving me the chance to coach at El Paso High School.

Thanks to Herman Masin, editor of Scholastic Coach, for all of his help and suggestions during the past 30 years.

Thanks to Dr. James A. Peterson for all of his help and encouragement.

CONTENTS

BEFORE WE BEGIN

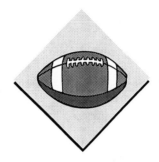

What You Will Find In This Book:

- A complete playbook for a variation of the split-4, which is referred to in this book as the *base*.

- A system that enables any coach to create over one hundred variations of the *base*.

- Straight talk about how to stop the option, not just a narrative of the "old assignments" that never really worked.

- The assignments and techniques necessary to play both man and zone pass coverage.

- One dozen innovative stunt tactics.

- 101 explosive stunts from a variety of man and zone pass coverages.

- Special strategies versus the aceback and empty formations.

A few terms will constantly be referred to throughout the text. Because different phrases/words can sometimes mean different things to different people, the following terms are defined and clarified as they are used in this book:

- **Strongside/weakside:** The strongside is toward the tight end, and the weakside is toward the split end. Strong defenders (example: strong tackle) are aligned on the tight-end side, and weak defenders are aligned on the split-end side.

- **Player position names** are illustrated in Figure Intro-1:

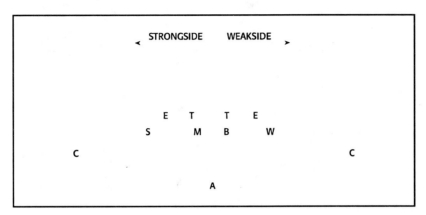

Figure Intro-1

Strong cornerback—the cornerback who lines up opposite the flanker.

Assassin—the free safety.

Stud—the outside linebacker who lines up toward the strongside.

Strong end—the defensive end who lines up on the strongside.

Strong tackle—the defensive tackle who lines up on the strongside.

Mike—the inside linebacker aligned on the strongside.

Buck—the inside linebacker aligned on the weakside.

Weak tackle—the defensive tackle who lines up on the weakside.

Weak end—the defensive end who lines up on the weakside.

Whip—the outside linebacker (strong-safety type of player) who lines up on the weakside.

Weak cornerback—The cornerback who lines up opposite the split end.

- Gap responsibilities are lettered as illustrated in Figure Intro-2:

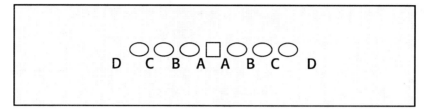

Figure Intro-2

- Alignments are numbered as illustrated in Figure Intro-3:

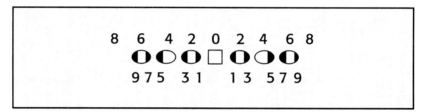

Figure Intro-3

- Receivers are numbered as illustrated in Figure Intro-4:

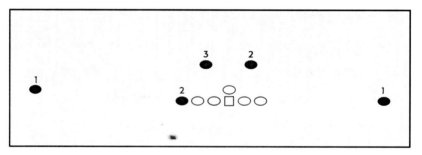

Figure Intro-4

CHAPTER 1

TWELVE INNOVATIVE STUNT TACTICS

New Defensive Strategies

In recent years, defensive coaches have developed a number innovative strategies that have made pass blocking a chaotic guessing game, destroyed the reliability of hot reads, and limited the number of pass receivers an offense can put into a pattern and still safely protect the quarterback. Most of these new strategies involve the tactic of illusion. When employing an illusion scheme, seven or eight defenders will attack the line of scrimmage at the snap, and give the offense the illusion of a total blitz. Once the defense reads pass, however, only a pre-determined number of defenders will continue to rush the quarterback. The remaining fake blitzers will either spy the running backs or drop off into coverage. To compound the offensive problem even further, the fake blitzers may be defensive linemen. Therefore, the offense never knows (until it is too late) how many or which defenders will rush the quarterback. Every defender aligned in the box is now both a potential pass rusher and a coverage player. Modern offenses must account for each and every player in the box. Illusion gives the defense a tremendous advantage over the offense and is not only an effective passing game deterrent, but it's also proven to be deadly versus the run. If, in future years, offensive teams try to counter illusion tactics by employing formations that feature no running backs, they will become one dimensional, and whenever an offense becomes one dimensional, it becomes easier to defend.

Illusion Stunts

Illusion stunts are the grandparents of the entire defensive revolution. Figure 1-1 shows eight defenders attacking the line at the snap. The offense's dilemma is trying to figure out which defenders are *spying* the two running backs—the outside linebackers, the inside linebackers, or the ends. It could actually be any of those defenders. If the tight end releases, the offense must attempt to block the *illusion* of eight pass rushers with seven blockers. If the offense tries to release the tight end and one or two running backs, it must attempt to block the *illusion* of an 8-on-6 or 8-on-5 mismatch, which often results in one, two, or three unblocked defenders chasing the quarterback. When this happens, the quarterback may be able to beat the sack, but he'll often end up throwing off balance, making a bad decision, and/or getting picked.

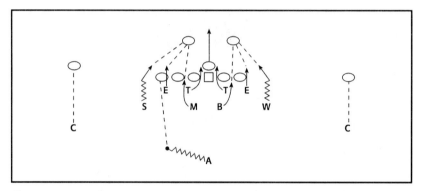

Figure 1-1

Banjo Blitzes

Most coaches refer to this tactic as a *zone blitz* or *fire zone blitz*. I call it banjo for several reasons. One reason is because when I first saw the tactic, it reminded me of the old strongside combo coverage, traditionally called *banjo*, that has been around for years. Another reason is because the cornerbacks are playing man, not zone. Back when Tom Bass was coaching in the NFL, he was blitzing linebackers and dropping linemen into pass coverage. Because every defender dropping into coverage was employing zone techniques, Tom called the tactic *zone blitz*. Because I learned both the tactic and its name from Tom, I had to give the "new zone blitz" another name, *banjo*. Two innovations have been added to the old *banjo* concept to create the new scheme. First, a third defender has been added to the *banjo* scheme, and secondly, defensive linemen are now dropping off into *banjo* coverage. In Figure 1-2, eight defenders are attacking the line at the snap. Once they read pass, however, the strong end, Mike, and the weak end drop off into coverage. The defenders dropping into coverage are jointly responsible for covering the tight end and two running backs. Each defender is therefore responsible for covering any of these three receivers if they enter his zone. I will refer to the three *banjo* zones into which the defenders drop as: Abel, Baker, and Charlie.

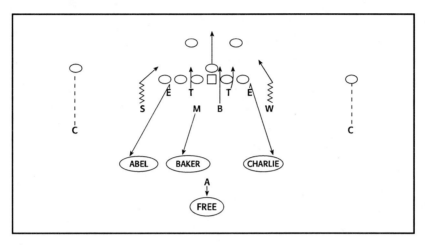

Figure 1-2

Gumbo Blitzes

This tactic is very similar to the old *banjo* concept in which two strongside defenders combo-covered the tight end and the strongside halfback by themselves. What's new about gumbo is that a weakside illusion is being employed and one defender is *spying* the weakside halfback instead of being assigned straight man coverage. Like *banjo*, *gumbo* holds the offense accountable for blocking all of the potential pass rushers in the box. It also causes offensive linemen to frequently end up blocking "air," and eliminates double-read pass-blocking schemes. In Figure 1-3 the strong end and Mike drop off into *gumbo* coverage and combo-cover the tight end and strong halfback, while the weak end *spies* the weak halfback.

Zone Blitzes

This tactic closely resembles the zone blitz of Tom Bass. Figure 1-4 shows Stud and the two inside linebackers blitzing while the strong end and two tackles drop off into coverage.

Delayed Overloads

Overload blitzes always have been, and always will be, an extremely effective defensive tactic. Overloads attempt to get more pass rushers on one side of the ball than

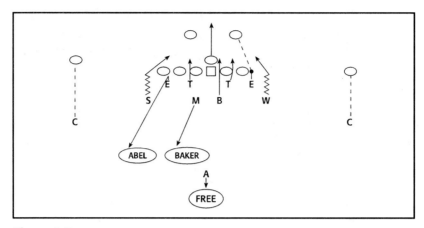

Figure 1-3

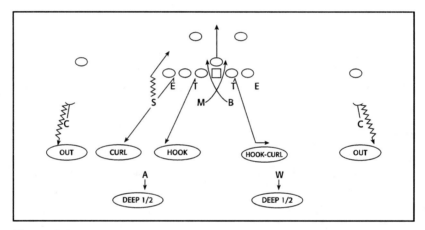

Figure 1-4

available offensive pass blockers. Figure 1-5 shows an overload with four strongside pass rushers. The only way that the offense can handle this overload is to use both their tight end and strongside halfback as pass blockers. The stunt begins as a strongside *illusion* with both ends *spying* the two halfbacks. Buck employs a base read technique versus run, but once he reads pass, he delay blitzes through the B gap.

Alignment Overload Blitzes

In addition to having a linebacker delay blitz, a defense can achieve an overload through its alignment. Figure 1-6 shows a weakside overload that is accomplished by the Assassin's fake weakside blitz.

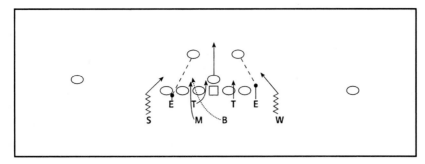

Figure 1-5

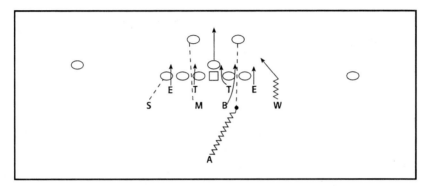

Figure 1-6

Line Twists

Line twists are particularly effective versus man pass-blocking assignments. They also enable seven defenders to drop off into coverage. Figure 1-7 shows a delayed line twist. In this stunt, the tackles and ends employ a base-read technique versus run. After they engage their respective blockers and read pass, they then twist. The tackles go under the ends and contain the quarterback, while the ends twist into the B gaps. Another type of line twist, in which the defenders will immediately twist at the snap of the ball, is generally more effective versus run. Line twists can also be combined with linebacker blitzes to intensify the pressure of a stunt.

Dogs

Most coaches refer to five-man pass rushes as dogs. This is an "old school" tactic that should still be included in every coach's blitz package. Figure 1-8 shows every player employing a base read except Stud, who covers the tight end, and Whip, who blitzes. Mike and Buck cover the running backs versus pass.

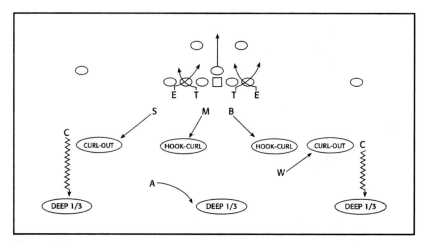

Figure 1-7

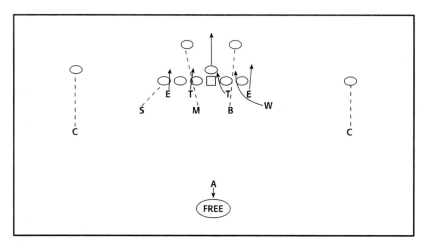

Figure 1-8

Blitzes

Any six-man rush is generally referred to as a blitz. These are more risky than dogs, because the defense is not afforded the luxury of a free safety. In Figure 1-9, Stud and Whip are blitzing, and the two inside linebackers are covering the two backs versus pass.

Flow Dogs

A flow dog is another "old school" tactic. In Figures 1-10a through 1-10c, both inside linebackers are assigned to blitz, but where they will blitz is predicated upon the backfield flow.

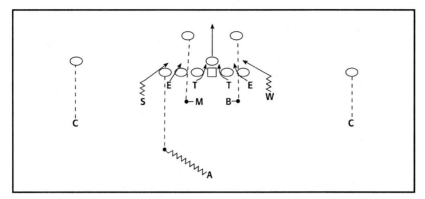

Figure 1-9

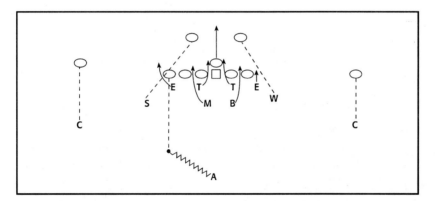

Figure 1-10a

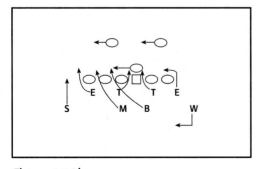

Figure 1-10b

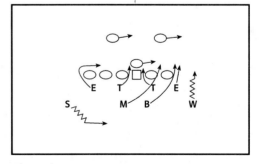

Figure 1-10c

Secondary Blitzes

Secondary blitzes and fake secondary blitzes are powerful, multifaceted weapons. Figure 1-11 shows a strong cornerback blitz, using a variation of cover 1. The stunt is enhanced by the weakside line twist.

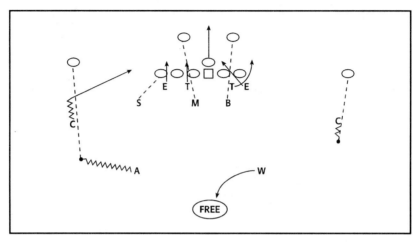

Figure 1-11

Twin Stunts

Whenever two players stunt through the same gap, it is referred to as a *twin stunt*. Figure 1-12 shows both the weak end and the weak tackle stunting through the B gap. This is an unusual tactic. Since few offensive teams ever see this type of stunt, it is often very effective. Twin stunts are usually called in passing situations.

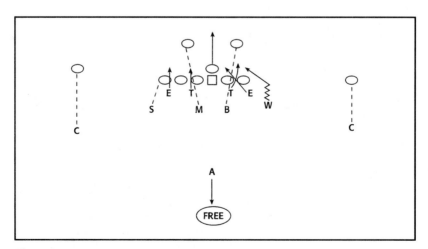

Figure 1-12

CHAPTER 2

BASE TECHNIQUES OF THE 44 DEFENSE

MIKE AND BUCK–BASE TECHNIQUE

Stance and Alignment

Players in the Mike and Buck positions should:

- Line up in a two-point stance, 4-to-5 yards from the ball.

- Position their outside foot to split the offensive guard's stance.

- Set up with their feet shoulder width apart and their weight on the balls of their feet.

- Start out in a good, low-hitting position that allows them to move laterally without having to raise or lower their body.

Position Responsibilities

- *Versus a run to their side:* If the play is outside of the defender, he attacks the B gap. He should expect to be blocked by the guard (fold), the tackle (kiss), or the lead back. He should attack the blocker and pursue the ballcarrier from an inside-out position. If the play is directed at the defender's A gap (trap or iso), he should fill the gap, attack the blockers, and make the tackle.

- *Versus a run to the opposite side:* The defender should attack the play-side A gap, check for counter or cutback, and then pursue the ballcarrier from an inside-out position.

- *Versus a pass to their side:* Responsibility depends upon stunt and coverage.

- *Versus a pass to the opposite side:* Responsibility depends upon stunt and coverage.

- *Versus a dropback pass:* Responsibility depends upon stunt and coverage.

Keys

Mike and Buck key the backfield flow through the near guard and center.

Techniques and Reactions

RUNNING PLAYS DIRECTED INTO THE A GAP

ISO (Figure 2-1)*:*

Playside linebacker: Fills the hole quickly. Attacks the fullback, as close to the line of scrimmage as possible, with an inside forearm rip. Dumps the fullback inside and maintains outside leverage.

Backside linebacker: Attacks the center and squeezes the play inside. Keeps his shoulders parallel to the line.

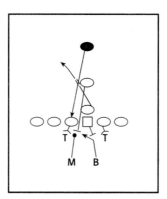

Figure 2-1

TRAP:

This play can be blocked in a number of ways. The following are some of the most common blocking schemes used to engineer trap plays:

Trap Scheme #1 (Figure 2-2)

Playside linebacker: When he sees the guard cross his face to block the other linebacker, he should immediately fill the A gap. This will enable him to avoid the tackle's block and tackle the fullback in the backfield.

Backside linebacker: Attacks the guard and squeezes the play inside. Maintains outside leverage.

Trap Scheme #2 (Figure 2-3)

Playside linebacker: Steps toward the B gap. When he realizes that the blocking scheme is not a fold because the tackle is attempting to block him, he should immediately fill the A gap.

Backside linebacker: Attacks the center and squeezes the play inside.

Trap Scheme #3 (Figure 2-4)

Playside linebacker: When he sees the guard cross his face to block the other linebacker, he should immediately fill the A gap and meet the tackle with an inside forearm.

Backside linebacker: Attacks the guard and squeezes the play inside. Maintains outside leverage.

Figure 2-2

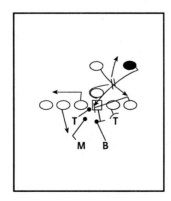
Figure 2-3

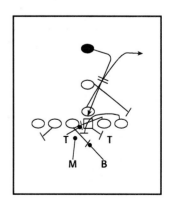
Figure 2-4

RUNNING PLAYS DIRECTED INTO THE B OR C GAPS

B GAP ISO (Figure 2-5):

Playside linebacker: Scrapes into the B gap. Attacks the fullback with an inside forearm rip and maintains outside leverage. Forces the ballcarrier to run inside.

Backside linebacker: Attacks the playside A gap. If he can beat the guard and penetrate into the backfield, he should do it. If not, he pursues down the line, maintaining inside-out leverage on the ballcarrier. Checks for counter and cutback.

C GAP POWER(Figure 2-6):

Playside linebacker: Attacks the guard with an outside forearm rip. Keeps his shoulders square to the line of scrimmage and maintains inside-out leverage on the ballcarrier.

Backside linebacker: Attacks the playside A gap. Penetrates the line if he can beat the guard; otherwise, he continues shuffling down the line while checking for counter and cutback. Keeps his shoulders parallel to the line and maintains inside-out position on the ball.

B GAP DIVE (Figure 2-7):

Playside linebacker: Scrapes to the outside shoulder of the tackle and attacks him with an inside forearm rip. Maintains outside leverage and keeps his shoulders parallel to the line.

Backside linebacker: Attacks the play-side A gap. Penetrates the line if he can beat the guard; otherwise, he continues shuffling down the line while checking for counter and cutback. Keeps his shoulders parallel to the line and maintains inside-out position on the ball.

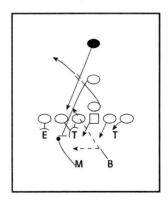

Figure 2-5

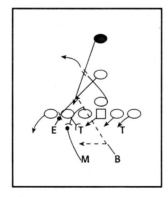

Figure 2-6

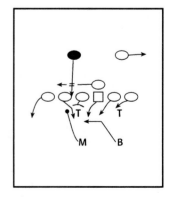

Figure 2-7

OUTSIDE RUNNING PLAYS (Figure 2-8)

Playside linebacker: Slides laterally while keeping his shoulders square to the line of scrimmage. Pursues the ballcarrier from an inside-out position. It is imperative that he doesn't over-run the ballcarrier.

Backside linebacker: Shuffles down the line keeping his shoulders parallel to the line. He is responsible for counter and cutback.

RUNNING PLAYS THAT FEATURE MISDIRECTION (Figure 2-9)

When confronted with a misdirection play, both linebackers must hold their ground and not react until they are able to locate the ball. It is also important to remember that, as a key, a pulling guard takes precedence over backfield flow.

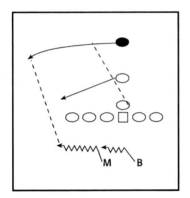 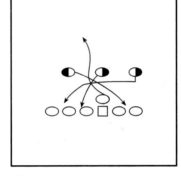

Figure 2-8   Figure 2-9

STUD AND WHIP'S 8 TECHNIQUE

Stance and Alignment

Players in the Stud and Whip positions should:

- Line up in a two-point stance with their shoulders parallel to the line.

- Set up with their outside foot at a slight stagger and their weight on the balls of their feet.

- Adjust their alignment depending upon field position, down and distance, and offensive tendencies. Generally, they will line up two yards from the tight end and two yards deep, but this may be extended as far as five yards. If there is no tight end, they should follow the same rule using the offensive tackle as their landmark.

Position Responsibilities

- *Versus a run to their side:* The defender must contain, since he is the primary force.
- *Versus a run to the opposite side:* The defender folds back and checks counter, cutback, and reverse.
- *Versus a pass to their side:* Depends upon stunt and coverage.
- *Versus a pass to the opposite side:* Depends upon stunt and coverage.
- *Versus a dropback pass:* Depends upon stunt and coverage.

Keys

Stud and Whip key the near back through the tight end.

Techniques and Reactions

D GAP OFF-TACKLE RUN (Figure 2-10)

Stud and Whip players should:

- React to the tight end's down block by coming up and attacking the fullback at the line. Close tight to the tight end's block and squeeze the play inside without penetrating the backfield and opening up a funnel for the ballcarrier.
- Attack the fullback with an inside forearm rip, and keep their pads lower than the fullback's pads.
- Keep their shoulders square to the line and their outside foot back as they make contact with the fullback.
- Maintain outside leverage and be prepared to react outside if the ballcarrier bounces the play outside.
- Never get hooked or cut.

C GAP OFF-TACKLE RUN (Figure 2-11)

Stud and Whip players must:

- Hold their ground and attack the tight end with an inside forearm rip.
- Maintain outside leverage and keep the ballcarrier to the inside.
- Tackle the ballcarrier from an outside-in position as he breaks the line of scrimmage.
- Always anticipate that the ballcarrier will bounce the play outside.
- Never get hooked or cut.

TWO-BACK SWEEPS (Figure 2-12)

Against two-back sweeps, Stud and Whip must:

- Squeeze the running lane.

- Attack the fullback at the line of scrimmage, aiming for his outside pad with their inside forearm rip.

- Stay lower than the fullback and keep their outside leg back and free.

- Want to force the ballcarrier inside or wide and deep.

- Never get hooked or cut.

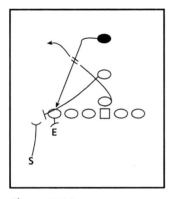
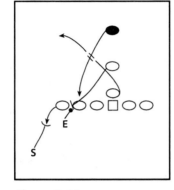
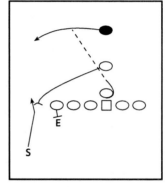

Figure 2-10   **Figure 2-11**   **Figure 2-12**

ACEBACK SWEEP (Figure 2-13)

As they recognize the backfield flow, Stud and Whip must:

- Immediately move toward the line and attack the tight end.

- Rip through the tight end's outside shoulder with an inside forearm rip and fight upfield.

- Restrict the running lane and force the play wide and deep.

- Maintain outside leverage.

INSIDE PLAYS (Figure 2-14)

Stud and Whip must:

- Hold their ground and be prepared for the ballcarrier to bounce the play inside.

- Maintain outside leverage and attack the ballcarrier from an outside-in position as he crosses the line of scrimmage. If there is not a tight end on their side of the field, and they are able to attack the ballcarrier in the backfield for a loss, they should do so.

FLOW AWAY (Figure 2-15)

The defenders should:

- First look for a reverse, bootleg, waggle or a throwback pass. They can use the near tackle's block as a helpful key.

- Adjust their pursuit angle and work downfield if they are threatened outside.

- Fold behind the defensive end and shuffle down the line looking for a cutback when they are sure there is no outside threat.

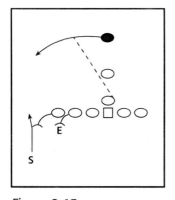

Figure 2-13

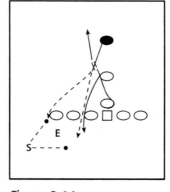

Figure 2-14

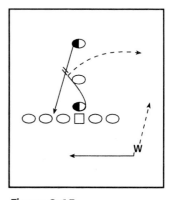

Figure 2-15

DEFENSIVE END'S 7 TECHNIQUE

Stance and Alignment

Defensive end should:

Line up inside shade on the tight end in a 3- or 4-point stance.

- Line up with his depth no deeper than 18".

- Line up within arms length of the offensive tackle when there is no tight end on his side.

Position Responsibilities

- *Versus a run* to his side: His primary responsibility is the C gap.

- *Versus a run* to the opposite side: He chases the play as deep as the ball.

- *Versus a pass* to his side: He rushes and contains the quarterback unless the coverage dictates otherwise.

- *Versus a pass* to the opposite side: He chases and contains the quarterback unless the coverage dictates otherwise.

- *Versus a dropback pass:* He rushes and contains the quarterback unless the coverage dictates otherwise.

Keys

First the tight end (pressure), then the near back (visual), and then a pulling lineman.

Techniques and Reactions

Defensive end should:

- Step with his outside foot and get his hands on the tight end.

- Not allow the tight end to release inside and block an inside linebacker.

WHEN THE TIGHT END BLOCKS

Defensive end should:

- Not get driven backwards or laterally, however, it is better to get driven backwards than laterally.

- Hang tough in the C gap and locate the ball.

  Inside play (Figure 2-16):

  He controls the tight end, plugs the C gap, and makes the tackle, using caution not to commit inside too quickly.

  Outside play (Figure 2-17):

  He works across the tight end's face and pursues the ball from an inside-out position.

WHEN THE TIGHT END RELEASES

  Versus a pass (Figure 2-18):

  He rushes and contains the quarterback unless stunt or coverage dictates otherwise.

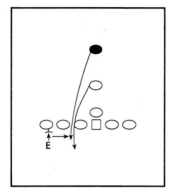

Figure 2-16

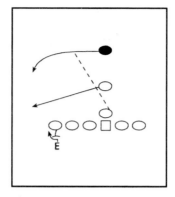

Figure 2-17

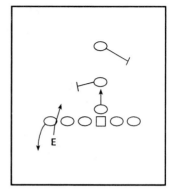

Figure 2-18

Versus a play going the opposite direction:

- No bootleg (Figure 2-19)

  He chases the play flat down the line of scrimmage, checking for counters, reverses, and cutbacks. He should never overrun the ball.

- Bootleg (Figure 2-20)

  He checks the quarterback unless the game plan dictates otherwise.

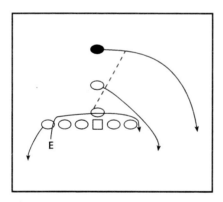

Figure 2-19

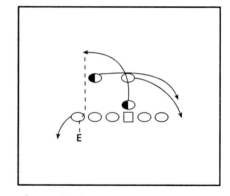

Figure 2-20

- Near back or lineman kick out (Figures 2-21a and 2-21b)

  He squeezes the C gap and closes the hole. He keeps his outside leg back and doesn't allow the blocker to hook him in. He attacks the blocker with his inside forearm. He should expect the ballcarrier to break the play outside.

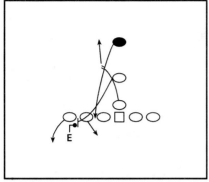

Figure 2-21a

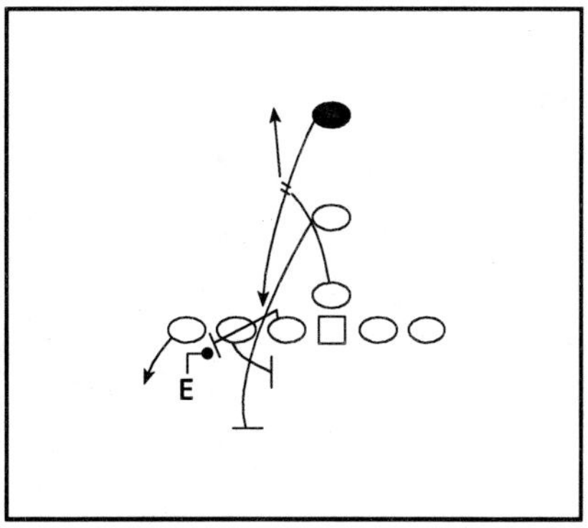

Figure 2-21b

- Near back or lineman hook block (Figures 2-22a and 2-22b)

    He squeezes the C gap and closes the hole. Keeps his outside leg back. He cannot allow the blocker to hook him in. He should attack the blocker with his inside forearm, force the play wide and deep, and pursue from an inside-out position.

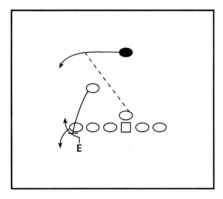

Figure 2-22a

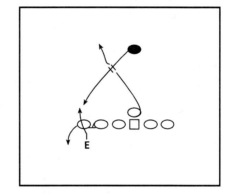

Figure 2-22b

DEFENSIVE TACKLE'S 3 TECHNIQUE

Stance and Alignment

Defensive tackle should:

- Line up on the line of scrimmage in a 3- or 4-point stance.

- Point his inside foot at the offensive guard's belt buckle, or align his inside foot slightly inside the guard's outside foot.

Keys

First the guard, then the tackle, and then the ball.

Position Responsibilities

- *Versus a run* to his side: He controls the B gap.

- *Versus a run* to the opposite side: He squeezes the A gap and then pursues.

- *Versus a pass:* He rushes.

- *Protecting Mike and Buck:* He doesn't allow the guard to get a free shot at the linebackers.

Important Techniques

Defensive tackle should:

- Keep his outside arm and leg free (maintain outside leverage).

- Keep his shoulders parallel to the line of scrimmage.

- Step with his inside foot and deliver a heavy, two-hand shiver to his primary key (in some situations he may want to use a forearm or shoulder technique).

Reactions

WHEN A GUARD BLOCKS THE DEFENSIVE TACKLE

- *Drive block* (Figure 2-23)

  If the guard's head gives the defensive tackle no key, the defender must control the guard's outside shoulder and squeeze the A gap, while still remembering that his primary responsibility is the B gap. He should maintain outside leverage, locate the ball, shed the blocker, and make the tackle.

- *Hook block* (Figure 2-24)

  The defensive tackle fights through the pressure and finds the ball. He keeps his feet back and the blocker away from his body. He slides to the outside and stays square to the line of scrimmage. He should maintain outside leverage and prevent the blocker's head from getting outside of him.

- *Turn-out block* (Figure 2-25)

  The defensive tackle controls the blocker and squeezes the A gap with the blocker's body. He keeps square to the line of scrimmage and doesn't fight inside too fast, or the back may break outside of him. He should remember that he's responsible for the B gap. He maintains outside leverage, locates the ball and pursues. He should not run around the block.

- *Double team* (Figure 2-26)

  The defensive tackle turns his shoulders to the drive blocker (the tackle) and releases pressure on the post block (the guard) by throwing his inside arm to the sky. He then drops his outside hip, squirms through the B gap, and splits the double team. He should get to the ground and keep his feet moving. He must hold his position and not get driven back or caved inside. He should not run around the block, he must tie up two blockers. If necessary, he should drop his outside leg and roll to the outside.

- *Combo (Kiss) block* (Figure 2-27)

  The defensive tackle must not drop to the ground, but use a knee drop instead of a hip drop, and attack the tackle with his outside arm and shoulder. He should not allow himself to get knocked backward; instead, he must hold his ground and force a true double team.

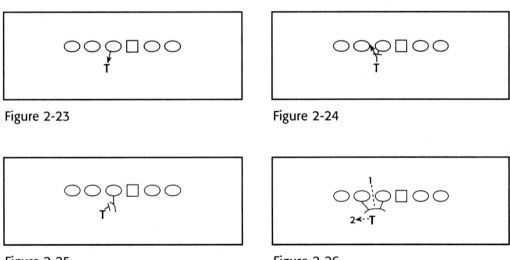

Figure 2-23   Figure 2-24

Figure 2-25   Figure 2-26

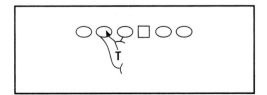

Figure 2-27

WHEN A GUARD BLOCKS INSIDE

- *Offensive tackle cracks on the defensive tackle* (Figure 2-28)

  The defender jams the guard. He must not let him get a free shot at an inside linebacker. He holds his ground and makes sure that he does not get driven back or to the side. If he's beaten the offensive tackle's head across the line of scrimmage, he should penetrate and pursue. If not, he flattens through the tackle and pursues. He fights the pressure of the blocker by keeping his shoulders square and staying low.

- *Offensive tackle cuts the defensive tackle off* (Figure 2-29)

  The defensive tackle jams the guard and keeps him off Mike. He rips his outside arm through the tackle's head. His pursuit is flat down the line, watching for cutbacks.

- *No outside pressure* (Figure 2-30)

  If the defensive tackle has no outside pressure, he is being trapped. He must close the A gap. He keeps his shoulders square to the line of scrimmage and maintains outside leverage as he squeezes the hole. He must be prepared for the ballcarrier to break the play outside. The tackle's normal technique is to attack the trapper with his inside forearm, but some game plans may dictate that he wrong-arm the trapper.

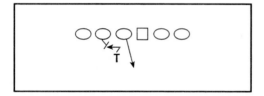

Figure 2-28

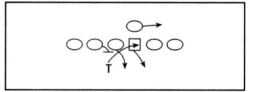

Figure 2-29

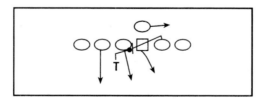

Figure 2-30

WHEN A GUARD PULLS OUTSIDE

- *Fold block* (Figure 2-31)

  If the defensive tackle has beaten the offensive tackle's head across the line of scrimmage, he then penetrates and pursues. If not, he flattens through the tackle and pursues. He must fight the pressure of the blocker by keeping his shoulders square and staying low.

- *No outside pressure* (Figure 2-32)

  The tackle should know that this is a trap, and play it as he did the previous trap.

WHEN A GUARD PULLS INSIDE

- *Offensive tackle cuts the defensive tackle off* (Figure 2-33)

  The defender should try to avoid contact with the offensive tackle. He should get into the guard's hip pocket and follow him to the point of attack.

- *When the center blocks the defensive tackle* (Figure 2-34)

  The defender flattens through the face of the center and takes the proper angle of pursuit.

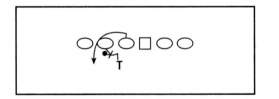

Figure 2-31

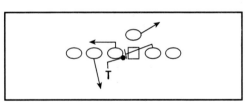

Figure 2-32

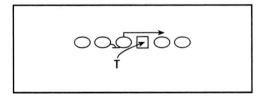

Figure 2-33

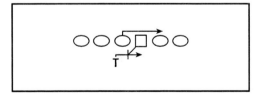

Figure 2-34

CREATING MULTIPLE FRONTS

When a team frequently stunts, it's of little consequence where the defensive players initially line up. What's important is where they are when the ball is snapped. You can create over 100 variations of your base defense with a very simple system. This system designates team alignments by using two digit number codes. You can align your tackles and inside linebackers in nine ways. These variations are designated by the first digit of the two-digit code, and are illustrated in Figures 2-35a through 2-35i.

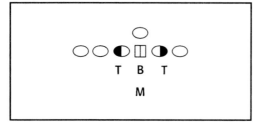

Figure 2-35a: 11, 13, 14, 15, 19

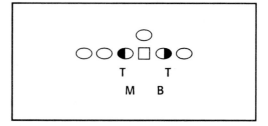

Figure 2-35b: 20's

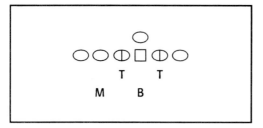

Figure 2-35c: 30's

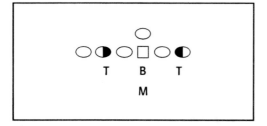

Figure 2-35d: 40's

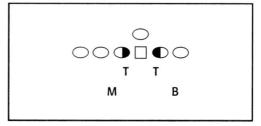

Figure 2-35e: 50's

Figure 2-35f: 60's

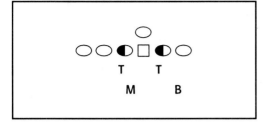

Figure 2-35g: 70's

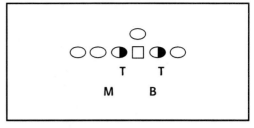

Figure 2-35h: 80's

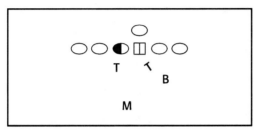

Figure 2-35i: 90's

The nine ways in which you can align the ends and outside linebackers are designated by the second digit of the code, and are shown in Figures 2-36a through 2-36i.

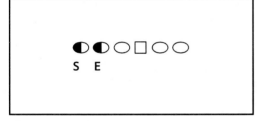

Figure 2-36a: One

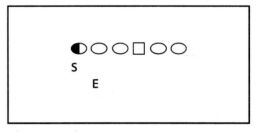

Figure 2-36b: Two

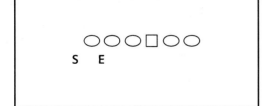

Figure 2-36c: Three

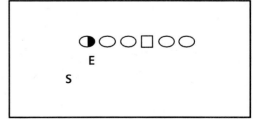

Figure 2-36d: Four

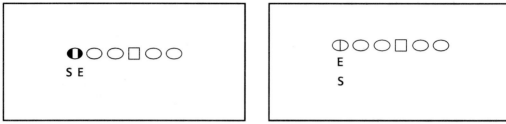

Figure 2-36e: Five   Figure 2-36f: Six

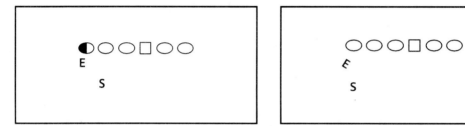

Figure 2-36g: Seven   Figure 2-36h: Eight

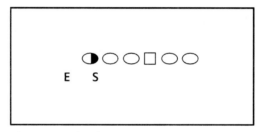

Figure 2-36i: Nine

Figures 2-37a through 2-37i show how you can create nine variations of a 40 front using this two-digit code system.

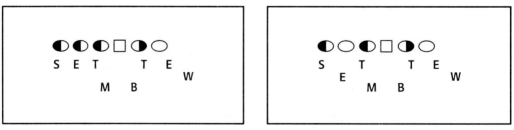

Figure 2-37a: 41   Figure 2-37b: 42

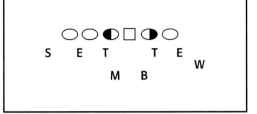

Figure 2-37c: 43

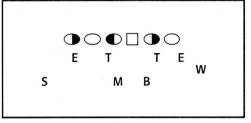

Figure 2-37d: 44

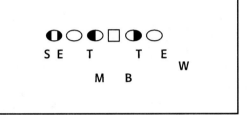

Figure 2-37e: 45

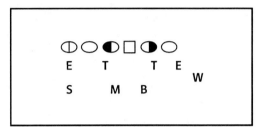

Figure 2-37f: 46

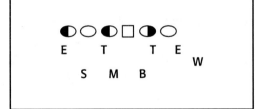

Figure 2-37g: 47

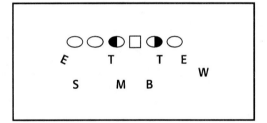

Figure 2-37h: 48

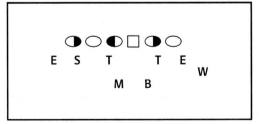

Figure 2-37i: 49

In addition to this two-digit system, you can create additional variations by aligning the Whip in five different positions. These five positions are assigned a letter designation. Figures 2-38a through 2-38e show these five positions.

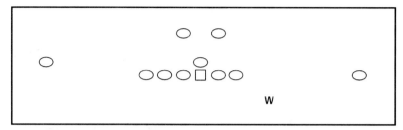

Figure 2-38a: Normal Position

Line up 2-5 yards outside of the defensive end, and on the line to five yard deep (also referred to as an 8 technique).

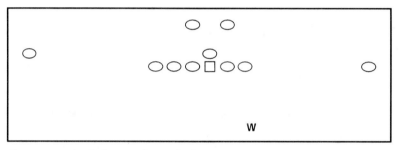

Figure 2-38b: "H" or Hole Technique

Line up shading the outside shoulder of the offensive tackle 4 1/2-6 yards deep.

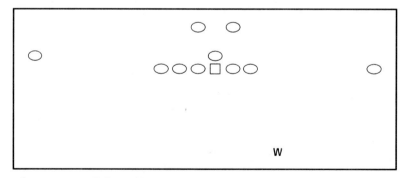

Figure 2-38c: "S" Position

Line up in a free safety position 7-12 yards deep.

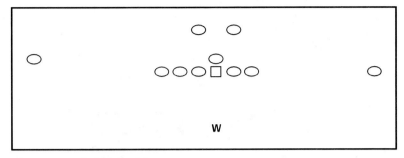

Figure 2-38d: "C" Position

Line up directly in front of the center, 5 1/2-6 1/2 yards deep.

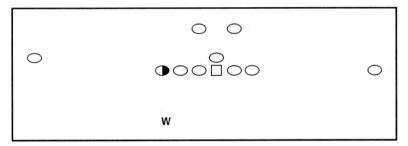

Figure 2-38e: "T" Position

Line up inside shade of the tight end 4-5 yards deep.

CHAPTER 3

HOW TO STOP
THE OPTION

In the late '60's or early '70's, Ara Parsegian, Notre Dame's head coach, referred to the *split defense* as the "national defense" at an AFCA convention. The split was the hottest thing in college football back then. However, five or six years later, the split had almost completely vanished from the college scene. How does a defense go from being the "national defense" to near extinction in such a short period of time? The answer is simple—the wishbone and the split-back veer offenses had rendered it useless.

Somewhere, for some insane reason, it seems that someone had inscribed in granite that there was only one way to stop the option. That way was to assign the pitch to the outside linebackers; the quarterback to the defensive ends; and the dive to the inside linebackers and tackles. Unfortunately, a lot of coaches accepted this as dogma. Amazingly, a lot of coaches still believe it!

Most of the coaches who were running the split defense at that time found out the hard way that these rigid assignments didn't work. As a result, most of the coaches pragmatically dumped the split defense and grasped for everything and anything that might work. Many coaches jumped aboard the 5-2 defense bandwagon. After all, this was the defense that had stopped the split-T. Those coaches who switched to the 5-2 quickly became content and secure again because this defense proved to be a very effective option deterrent. The defensive alignment, however, had little to do with its success. The 5-2 gurus of that era were some very bright, innovative men whose wisdom far surpassed many coaches who were using the split. Instead of giving every defender one rigid option assignment, as split coaches had done, the 5-2 coaches gave their players flexible assignments that changed according to the option type and its blocking scheme. For example, a 5-2 outside linebacker was responsible for the quarterback versus the inside veers, but versus the outside veers he was responsible for the dive. If the split coaches had evolved their assignments in this manner, perhaps their defense would have remained the "national defense." Today, in college football, the pass is *in* and the option is *out*; consequently, the split is *in*. History proves, however, that what's *in* and what isn't goes in cycles. Hopefully, when the present cycle is completed and the option returns, the split coaches will have learned from the past.

Before getting into the specifics of flexible option assignments, three coaching points should be mentioned.

- A team can't become proficient at stopping the option in a few days. The option is one of football's most potent weapons, and a well-coached option team can be a deadly nemesis. A team needs to practice their defense against the option a few days *each week*—even though it may not be playing an option team that week. This is a point that cannot be compromised.

- Align Mike and Buck five yards deep versus an option team. At this depth, they will have great angles and make big plays. If they start creeping toward the line of scrimmage, a good option team will easily wall them off. This may sound like a minor point, but it isn't.

- Versus an option team, it is preferable to line up the Stud on the line in a loose 8 technique and have the strong end play in the C gap.

Football has so many different types of options that an entire book could be devoted to that topic alone. This chapter discusses the strongside assignments for the inside veer, the outside veer, and the speed option. Understanding how to defend these three options will give any coach enough knowledge to easily create flexible assignments that will stop any variation of the option that he may encounter. It should be noted that although these assignments are illustrated utilizing zero coverage, they can easily be incorporated into any coverage.

DEFENDING THE VEER (Figures 3-1a and 3-1b)

Stud

Defender should:

- Feather the pitch.

- Key the tight end, and as the receiver releases, sink 1 1/2 yards off of the line and get his feet moving.

- Not ride the tight end too far outside—the angle of his sink should be almost straight back.

- Be ready to get his hands up to deflect a dump pass to the tight end as the defender sinks.

- Make it look as though he's playing the quarterback, but once the pitchback gets even with him, he should play that player (the exception being if Stud realizes that he is the last line of defense, then he must play the quarterback first and the pitch second).

Strong end

Defender should:

- Read the offensive tackle's head.
  - If the tackle tries to block him, he fights pressure and gets to a point that will enable him to force the quarterback to pitch quickly.
  - If the tackle blocks inside, the defender immediately calls "down-down" and tries to jam the tackle with his inside hand.

- Penetrate the line and attack the dive at the mesh point in the backfield.

- Force the quarterback to run the option downhill.

Mike

Defender should:

- Key the near back.
  - If he reads veer, he begins his scrape toward the B gap.
  - If he hears "down-down," he widens his angle and slow plays the quarterback.
  - If he doesn't hear "down-down," he attacks the dive at the line of scrimmage.

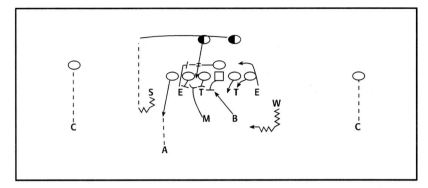

Figure 3-1a

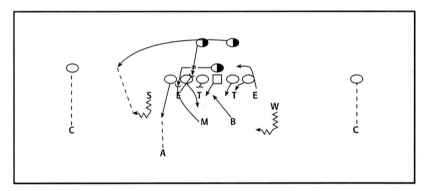

Figure 3-1b

DEFENDING THE OUTSIDE VEER (Figure3-2)

Stud

Defender should:

- Key the tight end. If he reads the tight end's down block, he calls "down-down" and closes hard inside.

- Attack the dive back at the mesh in the backfield and force the quarterback to run downhill.

Strong end

Defender should:

- Hold his ground and not allow himself to get driven inside.

- Fight upfield and try to force the play downhill.

Mike

Defender should:

- Key the halfback and read his angle. He naturally scrapes wider because of the halfback's angle. When Mike hears "down-down" his angle becomes even wider.

- Quickly check for a delayed pass to the tight end as he slow plays the quarterback.

Assassin

Defender should:

- Slow play the pitch. As he approaches the line, he quickly checks the tight end for a delayed pass.

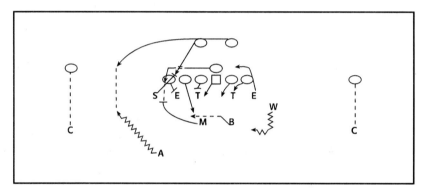

Figure 3-2

DEFENDING THE SPEED OPTION (Figure 3-3)

Stud

Defender should:

- Key the tight end. As he reads the tight end's down block, he calls "down-down" and closes hard to the inside.

- Attack the quarterback and force him to pitch quickly.

Strong end

Defender must:

- Hold his ground and not allow himself to get driven inside.

- Fight upfield and try to force the play downhill.

Mike

Defender should:

- Key the halfback and read his angle. He naturally scrapes wider because of the halfback's angle. When he hears "down-down" his angle becomes even wider.

- Quickly check for a delayed pass to the tight end as he jumps the pitch.

Assassin

Defender should:

- Slow play the pitch.

- Quickly check the tight end for a delayed pass as he approaches the line of scrimmage.

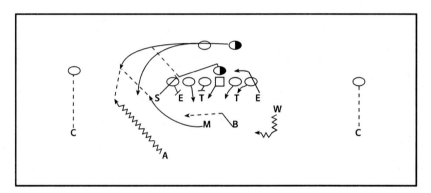

Figure 3-3

The first three of the following stunts illustrate three excellent change-ups that attack the option.

STUNT #1

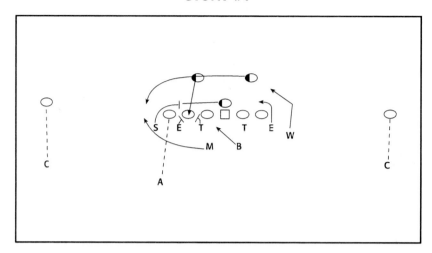

STUNT DESCRIPTION: This stunt has two important functions. First, it can quickly turn any option into an instant sweep. Second, it can take away the outside veer by creating havoc at the mesh point.

SECONDARY COVERAGE: Zero coverage. Mike and Buck cover the running backs versus pass.

STUD: Attacks the quarterback versus strongside option. Chases weakside option. Contains the quarterback versus pass.

STRONG END: Slants inside through the junction of the offensive tackle's neck and shoulder. Attacks the dive when flow is toward him. When flow is away, squeezes the play inside and chases.

STRONG TACKLE: Plays 3 technique.

MIKE: Scrapes outside and attacks the pitch versus strongside option. Fills the play-side A gap and looks for cutback versus weakside option. Covers the near back versus pass.

BUCK: Attacks the dive if not given a *"down-down"* call versus weakside option. If given a *"down-down"* call, attacks the quarterback. Covers the near back versus pass. Pusues strongside option from an inside-out position.

WEAK TACKLE: Plays 3 technique.

WEAK END: Reacts to the offensive tackle's block versus weakside option. If the tackle blocks inside, weak end calls *"down-down"* and attacks the dive back. If the tackle blocks him, he attacks the quarterback. Squeezes the play inside and chases versus strongside option.

WHIP: Attacks the pitch versus weakside option. Chases strongside option. Contains the quarterback versus pass.

ASSASSIN: Covers the tight end.

STRONG CORNER: Covers receiver #1 (inside technique).

WEAK CORNER: Covers receiver #1 (inside technique).

STUNT #2

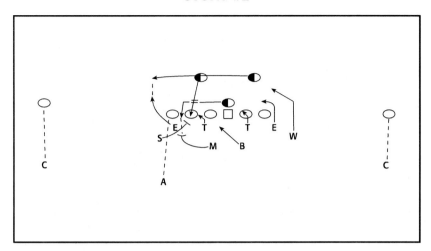

STUNT DESCRIPTION: The purpose of this stunt is to confuse both the offense's blocking assignments and the quarterback's read.

SECONDARY COVERAGE: Zero coverage. Mike and Buck cover the running backs versus pass.

STUD: Stunts through the junction of the offensive tackle's neck and shoulder. Attacks the dive when the option is to his side. Squeezes the play inside and chases when the option is away.

STRONG END: Slants outside and attacks the pitch versus strongside option. Chases weakside option. Contains the quarterback versus pass.

STRONG TACKLE: Plays 3 technique.

MIKE: Feathers the quarterback versus strongside option. Fills the playside A gap and looks for cutback versus weakside option. Covers the near back versus pass.

BUCK: Attacks the dive, if not given a *"down-down"* call versus weakside option. If given a *"down-down"* call, attacks the quarterback. Covers the near back versus pass.

WEAK TACKLE: Plays 3 technique.

WEAK END: Reacts to the offensive tackle's block versus weakside option. If the tackle blocks inside, weak end calls *"down-down"* and attacks the dive back. If the tackle blocks him, he attacks the quarterback. Squeezes the play inside and chases strongside option.

WHIP: Attacks the pitch versus weakside option. Chases strongside option. Contains the quarterback versus pass.

ASSASSIN: Covers the tight end.

STRONG CORNER: Covers receiver #1 (inside technique).

WEAK CORNER: Covers receiver #1 (inside technique).

STUNT #3

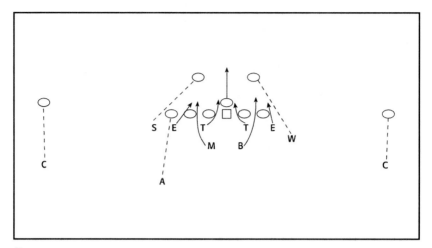

Pass

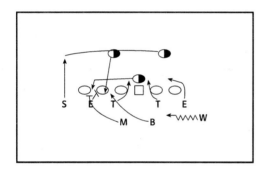

Strongside

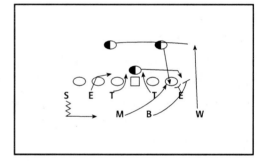

Weakside

STUNT DESCRIPTION: This is a flow dog. The two inside linebackers' blitz locations are predicated upon backfield flow.

SECONDARY COVERAGE: Zero coverage. Stud and Whip cover the near backs versus pass.

STUD: Lines up in an 8 technique on the line of scrimmage. Plays the pitch versus strongside option. Folds back and checks counter, cutback, and throwback versus weakside option. Covers the near back versus pass.

STRONG END: Lines up in the C gap and slants at the offensive tackle's outside shoulder. Plays the dive versus strongside option. Chases weakside option. Contains the quarterback versus pass.

STRONG TACKLE: Slants across the guard's face and controls the A gap.

MIKE: Scrapes into the C gap and tackles the quarterback versus strongside option. Scrapes into the weakside B gap and tackles the dive versus weakside option. Blitzes through the B gap versus pass.

BUCK: Scrapes into the C gap and tackles the quarterback versus weakside option. Scrapes into the strongside B gap and tackles the dive versus strongside option. Blitzes through the B gap versus pass.

WEAK TACKLE: Slants across the guard's face and controls the A gap.

WEAK END: Lines up in a tight 7 technique. Plays the dive versus weakside option. Chases strongside option. Contains the quarterback versus pass.

WHIP: Lines up in an 8 technique on the line of scrimmage. Plays the pitch versus weakside option. Folds back and checks counter, cutback, and throwback versus strongside option. Covers the near back versus pass.

ASSASSIN: Covers the tight end.

STRONG CORNER: Covers receiver #1 (inside technique).

WEAK CORNER: Covers receiver #1 (inside technique).

CHAPTER 4

BASIC PRINCIPLES
OF BLITZING

- If a player blitzes infrequently, using it as an element of surprise, it's important that he disguises his intention.

- If a player frequently blitzes, disguising his intention may not be as important because he may want to occasionally give the offense a false key by *showing blitz* but then *playing straight* at the snap of the ball. Whichever strategy he decides to use, it is important that he does not establish a pattern that can be exploited.

- A player's eyes are one of his most important tools when blitzing. To be an effective blitzer, a player must be able to see (on the run) the keys that will lead him to the ball. Seeing these keys is the first step in being able to read and react to them.

- Unless the blitz is a delayed reaction to a pass, it is critical that the blitzer is moving, attacking, and penetrating the line of scrimmage at the snap of the ball.

- Blitzers must keep their feet moving at all times. This factor is especially important when they become engaged with a blocker.

- A blitzing player should use his quickness to avoid blockers.

- If the play is a pass, and the blitzer becomes engaged with a blocker, he should keep his hands inside of the blocker's hands and try to maintain separation from the blocker. He should not look at the passer too soon because he might lose sight of the blocker. A blitzer must first defeat the blocker before he can sack the quarterback. While blitzers should have a predetermined pass rush move in mind, they should be ready to change their move according to the circumstance. Blitzers need to take what the blocker gives them and make their move at the appropriate time. Remember that if a blitzing player makes his pass rush move too soon, the blocker will have time to recover. On the other hand, if he makes his move too late, he will probably be too close to the blocker, thereby enabling the blocker to get into the blitzer's body and nullify his charge. If possible, a blitzer should try to get the blocker turned one way and then make his move in the opposite direction. The blitzing player should also, use his forward momentum to manipulate the blocker's momentum. If the blocker's momentum is back, the blitzer should attack him with a power move and knock him backwards. If his momentum is forward, the player can use a move that puts the blocker forward and destroys his balance. Blitzing players should never leave their feet to bat a ball down. They should get their hands up as the quarterback begins his throwing motion, but keep charging toward the quarterback. Too often, when a defender jumps up to bat a pass down, the quarterback will duck under, elude the defender, and scramble out of the pocket.

- If the play is a run, a blitzer should react to his keys and the pressure of blocks as he normally would if he were employing a read technique. Since a blitzer has forward momentum to his advantage, he should use his hands rather than his forearm when attacking a blocker. Blitzing players must maintain separation from blockers and not let them get into the blitzer's legs. If possible, the blitzer should try to make the blocker miss.

- When blitzing, a player should keep his body under control at all times, try to maintain a low center of gravity, and provide as small a target as possible for the blockers.

- Blitzers need to study their opponents' game films carefully. They should know how their potential blockers react and what techniques they favor. It helps to know the strengths and weaknesses of the opponent.

- Blitzers should also study the opponent's eyes as he's getting set at the line of scrimmage. The blocker's eyes will often tell the blitzer where he's going. Studying the pressure that the blocker puts on his down hand when he gets into his stances will also frequently give a pass/run or directional key.

- Blitzers who study the scouting report will increase their knowledge of the opponents' formation, down-and-distance, and field-position tendencies. They should use this information to anticipate, but never to guess.

- All players should gang tackle, and try to strip the ball out of the ballcarrier's arm. Players should never take for granted that a running back or quarterback has been downed. If they arrive at a pile late, they should be on the alert for a loose ball.

- Players must maintain total intensity from the time the ball is snapped until the whistle is blown.

- Before the snap, blitzers should anticipate potential blockers and be prepared to react to those blockers as they penetrate the line.

- On plays directed toward a blitzer's side of the field, he should make the tackle. On plays directed away from that player, he should take the proper angle of pursuit and be in on the tackle. Players should always pursue relentlessly. Remember that if a player is not within five yards of the ball when the whistle blows, he is probably loafing.

- If the backfield action does not indicate flow, a blitzer should protect his gap until he finds the ball. He should never guess.

- If a player is assigned to *spy* (cover a back) when he's blitzing, he should expect that the back will first block and then run a delayed route. Do not allow the defender to be fooled. Remind him that he must cover the back, no matter what the back does, until the whistle blows.

- The ball is the blitzers' trigger. When the ball is snapped, *they're gone*! They should not listen to an opponent's cadence; the quarterback is not talking to the blitzer!

Players should not rely upon the lines that are marked on the field. The ball, not the lines, establishes the line of scrimmage.

CHAPTER 5

ZERO COVERAGE STUNTS

When zero coverage is employed, the coverage has no free safeties. The three defensive backs are assigned to guard the tight end and two wide receivers man-to-man. One or two defenders in the box are assigned to cover the two running backs, and the fourth defensive back is either sent on a blitz or assigned to cover one of the running backs.

The strength of the zero coverage strategy is that it has eight defenders in the vicinity of the box, attacking gaps and penetrating the line of scrimmage. Its weakness is that all of the secondary defenders are locked on receivers and none are keying the ball; therefore, if a runner breaks the line of scrimmage or a defensive back gets beaten deep, there is a good chance that a touchdown will result. Despite its weakness, zero coverage can cause an offense a lot of problems, especially when the defenders in the box have some "quicks" and the defensive backs are skillful man-to-man pass defenders.

SECONDARY MAN-TO-MAN TECHNIQUES FOR ZERO COVERAGE

Stance and Alignment

A defensive secondary player should:

- Align himself with an inside shade on the receiver, approximately seven yards deep.

- Set up with a narrow base, feet inside the width of his armpits, outside foot up (toe-heel relationship).

- Keep his weight on his front foot.

- Keep his knees bent and his hips lowered.

- Slightly round his back with his head and shoulders over his front foot (nose over the toes).

- Allow his arms to hang loose.

- See both the receiver and the quarterback (with his peripheral vision).

Backpedal

A defensive secondary player should:

- Maintain inside leverage on the receiver.

- Keep a good forward lean as he backpedals (chin down and nose over the toes).

- Push off with his front foot and make his first step with his back foot. He should not step forward or lift a foot and set it back down in the same place.

- Keep his weight on the balls of his feet.

- Reach back with each step and pull his weight over his feet.

- Keep his feet close to the ground during the backpedal.

- Not over stride; take small-to-medium steps.

- Keep his arms bent at a 90-degree angle - relaxed, but pumping vigorously.

- Maintain a proper cushion. When the receiver gets 10 yards downfield, the defender should be 15 yards deep. When the receiver is 15 yards downfield, the defender should be 18 yards deep.

- Remember and anticipate that 3-step routes are usually thrown five-to-seven yards downfield (the exception being the fade); 5-step patterns are thrown eight-to-fifteen yards downfield; and 7-step routes are usually thrown eighteen or more yards downfield.

- Be aware of a receiver's split. Wide splits often indicate inside routes; tight splits often indicate outside routes.

- Keep his shoulders parallel to the line and not let the receiver turn him.

- Mirror the receiver's movements, while keeping his own outside shoulder on the receiver's inside shoulder. He must not let the receiver get head up with him.

- Control the speed of his back-pedal. When the receiver makes his break, the defender must be under control and able to gather and break quickly in the direction of the break.

- Concentrate on the base of the receiver's numbers until he makes his final break.

- Anticipate a break when the receiver changes his forward lean, begins to chop his feet, or begins to widen his base.

- Honor all inside fakes.

- Not backpedal at the snap if aligned on a tight end. Be ready to jump a flat or crossing route. If the tight end goes vertical, the defender must work to an inside leverage position.

- Remember that "if the receiver gets even (with him), he's leavin'." Whenever a receiver gets too close, the defender must turn and run with him, keeping his body between the receiver and the ball. He must not allow separation to occur. As he's running with the receiver, he can try to disrupt the receiver's strides by slapping at his near hand and wrist.

Plant and Drive

A defensive secondary player should:

- Drop his shoulder in the direction of the receiver's break, and explode in that direction when the receiver makes his final break. He must make his break parallel to the receiver's break, and quickly close the cushion.

- Not lose concentration on the receiver. He should not look for the ball until he's closed his cushion, and he sees the receiver look for the ball.

- Be in a position after he has begun his drive, so that the receiver will have to make contact with him in order to change directions.

Playing the Ball

A defensive secondary player should:

- Attack the ball at its highest point.

- Play the ball, not the receiver, when the ball is to his inside and the receiver is outside of him.

- Play the ball through the receiver's upfield shoulder when the receiver is between him and the ball. He should never cut in front of the receiver to make an interception unless he's absolutely sure that he can get two hands on the ball.

- Try to catch the ball or break up a pass with two hands, not one.

- Always knock the ball toward the ground, never up in the air.

- Try to strip the ball if the receiver catches the pass.

- Head to the nearest sideline when he intercepts a pass.

- Always look the ball into his hands and protect it after he catches it.

STUNT #4

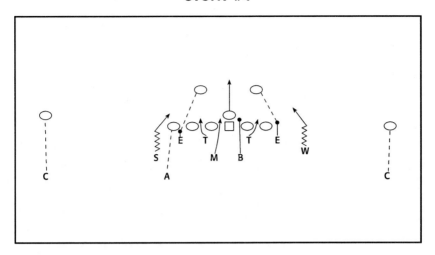

STUNT DESCRIPTION: This is an illusion stunt that gives the offense the *illusion* of an eight-man pass rush.

SECONDARY COVERAGE: Zero coverage. The ends spy the two running backs. Possible variation: assign the outside linebackers to spy and allow the two ends to rush.

STUD: Creeps toward the line during cadence and rushes from the edge. Contains pass and strongside run. Chases weakside run.

STRONG END: Plays 7 technique versus run. Draws the tackle's block and then spies the near back versus pass.

STRONG TACKLE: Stunts into the B gap.

MIKE: Blitzes through the A gap.

BUCK: Blitzes through the A gap.

WEAK TACKLE: Stunts into the B gap.

WEAK END: Plays 7 technique versus run. Draws the tackle's block and then spies the near back versus pass.

WHIP: Creeps toward the line during cadence and rushes from the edge. Contains pass and weakside run. Chases strongside run.

ASSASSIN: Covers the tight end.

STRONG CORNER: Covers receiver #1 (inside technique).

WEAK CORNER: Covers receiver #1 (inside technique).

STUNT #5

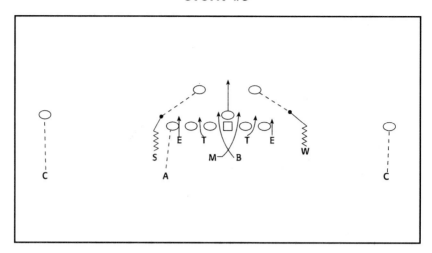

STUNT DESCRIPTION: This is an illusion stunt that gives the offense the *illusion* of an eight-man pass rush.

SECONDARY COVERAGE: Zero coverage. Stud and Whip spy the two running backs. Possible variation: assign the ends to spy and allow Stud and Whip to rush.

STUD: Creeps toward the line during cadence and gives the impression that he's rushing from the edge. Contains strongside run and chases weakside run. Spies the near back versus pass.

STRONG END: Plays 7 technique versus run. Contains the quarterback versus pass.

STRONG TACKLE: Stunts into the B gap.

MIKE: Blitzes through the weakside A gap. Buck goes first. Mike's first step is a short jab-step parallel to the line with his right foot.

BUCK: Blitzes through the strongside A gap. Buck goes first.

WEAK TACKLE: Stunts into the B gap.

WEAK END: Plays 7 technique versus run. Contains the quarterback versus pass.

WHIP: Creeps toward the line during cadence and gives the impression that he's rushing from the edge. Contains weakside run and chases strongside run. Spies the near back versus pass.

ASSASSIN: Covers the tight end.

STRONG CORNER: Covers receiver #1 (inside technique).

WEAK CORNER: Covers receiver #1 (inside technique).

STUNT #6

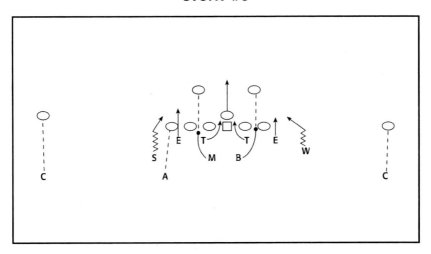

STUNT DESCRIPTION: This is an illusion stunt that gives the offense the *illusion* of an eight-man pass rush.

SECONDARY COVERAGE: Zero coverage. Mike and Buck spy the two running backs. Possible variation: assign either the two ends or the outside linebackers to spy, and allow Mike and Buck to rush.

STUD: Creeps toward the line during cadence and rushes from the edge. Contains strongside run and chases weakside run. Contains the quarterback versus pass.

STRONG END: Plays 7 technique.

STRONG TACKLE: Stunts into the A gap.

MIKE: Fakes a blitz toward the B gap. Secures the B gap versus run and spies the near back versus pass.

BUCK: Fakes a blitz toward the B gap. Secures the B gap versus run and spies the near back versus pass.

WEAK TACKLE: Stunts into the A gap.

WEAK END: Plays 7 technique.

WHIP: Creeps toward the line during cadence and rushes from the edge. Contains weakside run and chases strongside run. Contains the quarterback versus pass.

ASSASSIN: Covers the tight end.

STRONG CORNER: Covers receiver #1 (inside technique).

WEAK CORNER: Covers receiver #1 (inside technique).

STUNT #7

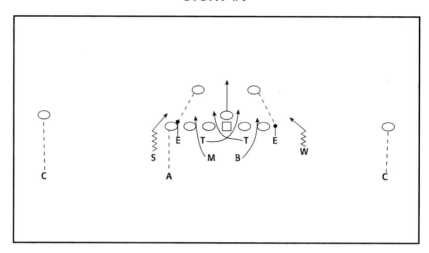

STUNT DESCRIPTION: This is an illusion stunt that gives the offense the *illusion* of an eight-man pass rush.

SECONDARY COVERAGE: Zero coverage. The ends spy the two running backs. Possible variation: assign either Mike and Buck, or the outside linebackers to spy and allow the ends to rush.

STUD: Creeps toward the line during cadence and rushes from the edge. Contains strongside run and chases weakside run. Contains the quarterback versus pass.

STRONG END: Plays 7 technique versus run. Spies the near back versus pass.

STRONG TACKLE: Stunts into the weakside A gap. The weak tackle goes first. Strong tackle makes his first step a short jab-step parallel to the line with his right foot to enable him to clear.

MIKE: Blitzes through the B gap.

BUCK: Blitzes through the B gap.

WEAK TACKLE: Stunts into the strongside A gap. Weak tackle goes first.

WEAK END: Plays 7 technique versus run. Spies the near back versus pass.

WHIP: Creeps toward the line during cadence and rushes from the edge. Contains weakside run and chases strongside run. Contains the quarterback versus pass.

ASSASSIN: Covers the tight end.

STRONG CORNER: Covers receiver #1 (inside technique).

WEAK CORNER: Covers receiver #1 (inside technique).

STUNT #8

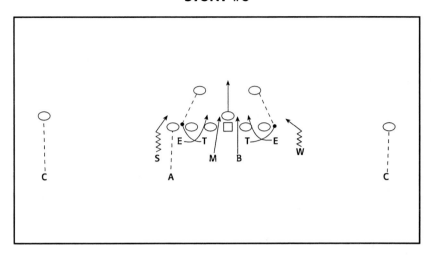

STUNT DESCRIPTION: This is an illusion stunt that gives the offense the *illusion* of an eight-man pass rush.

SECONDARY COVERAGE: Zero coverage. The tackles spy the two running backs. Possible variation: assign the outside linebackers to spy and allow the tackles to rush.

STUD: Creeps toward the line during cadence and rushes from the edge. Contains strongside run and chases weakside run. Contains the quarterback versus pass.

STRONG END: Twists with the tackle. The tackle goes first. Strong end's first step is a short jab-step parallel to the line with his right foot. He is responsible for securing the B gap.

STRONG TACKLE: Twists with the end. Strong tackle goes first. Slants across the face of the offensive tackle into the C gap. Secures the C gap versus run and spies the near back versus pass.

MIKE: Blitzes through the A gap.

BUCK: Blitzes through the A gap.

WEAK TACKLE: Twists with the end. Weak tackle goes first. Slants across the face of the offensive tackle into the C gap. Secure the C gap versus run and spies the near back versus pass.

WEAK END: Twists with the tackle. The weak tackle goes first. Weak end's first step is a short jab-step parallel to the line with his right foot. He is responsible for securing the B gap.

WHIP: Creeps toward the line during cadence and rushes from the edge. Contains weakside run and chases strongside run. Contains the quarterback versus pass.

ASSASSIN: Covers the tight end.

STRONG CORNER: Covers receiver #1 (inside technique).

WEAK CORNER: Covers receiver #1 (inside technique).

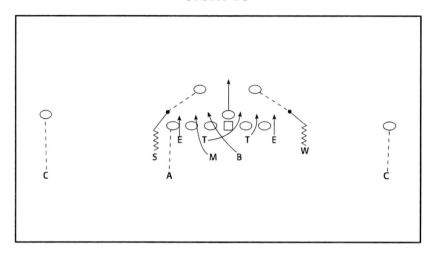

STUNT DESCRIPTION: This is an illusion stunt that gives the offense the *illusion* of an eight-man pass rush.

SECONDARY COVERAGE: Zero coverage. The outside linebackers spy the two running backs. Possible variation: assign the ends to spy and allow the outside linebackers to rush.

STUD: Creeps toward the line during cadence and gives the impression that he's rushing from the edge. Contains strongside run and chases weakside run. Spies the near back versus pass.

STRONG END: Plays 7 technique versus run. Contains the quarterback versus pass.

STRONG TACKLE: Slants across the center's face into the weakside A gap.

MIKE: Blitzes through the inside shoulder of the offensive tackle and secures the B gap.

BUCK: Blitzes through the strongside A gap.

WEAK TACKLE: Stunts into the B gap.

WEAK END: Plays 7 technique versus run. Contains the quarterback versus pass.

WHIP: Creeps toward the line during cadence and gives the impression that he's rushing from the edge. Contains weakside run and chases strongside run. Spies the near back versus pass.

ASSASSIN: Covers the tight end.

STRONG CORNER: Covers receiver #1 (inside technique).

WEAK CORNER: Covers receiver #1 (inside technique).

STUNT #10

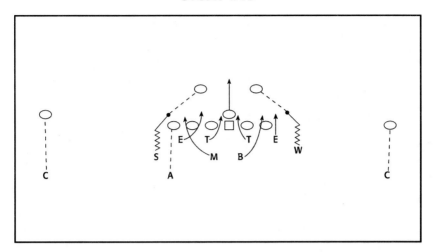

STUNT DESCRIPTION: This is an illusion stunt that gives the offense the *illusion* of an eight-man pass rush.

SECONDARY COVERAGE: Zero coverage. The outside linebackers spy the two running backs. Possible variation: assign Mike and the weak end to spy and allow the outside linebackers to rush.

STUD: Creeps toward the line during cadence and gives the impression that he's rushing from the edge. Contains strongside run and chases weakside run. Spies the near back versus pass.

STRONG END: Slants across the offensive tackle's face into the B gap.

STRONG TACKLE: Slants into and secures the A gap.

MIKE: Blitzes through the outside shoulder of the offensive tackle and secures the C gap. Contains the quarterback versus dropback pass.

BUCK: Blitzes through the B gap.

WEAK TACKLE: Slants into and secures the A gap.

WEAK END: Plays 7 technique versus run. Contains the quarterback versus pass.

WHIP: Creeps toward the line during cadence and gives the impression that he's rushing from the edge. Contains weakside run and chases strongside run. Spies the near back versus pass.

ASSASSIN: Covers the tight end.

STRONG CORNER: Covers receiver #1 (inside technique).

WEAK CORNER: Covers receiver #1 (inside technique).

STUNT #11

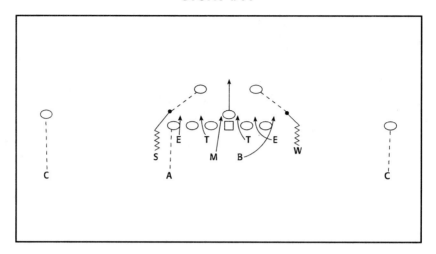

STUNT DESCRIPTION: This is an illusion stunt that gives the offense the *illusion* of an eight-man pass rush.

SECONDARY COVERAGE: Zero coverage. The outside linebackers spy the two running backs. Possible variation: assign Buck and the strong end to spy and allow the outside linebackers to rush.

STUD: Creeps toward the line during cadence and gives the impression that he's rushing from the edge. Contains strongside run and chases weakside run. Spies the near back versus pass.

STRONG END: Plays 7 technique versus run. Contains the quarterback versus pass.

STRONG TACKLE: Slants into and secures the B gap.

MIKE: Blitzes through the A gap.

BUCK: Blitzes through the outside shoulder of the offensive tackle and secures the C gap. Contains the quarterback versus drop-back pass.

WEAK TACKLE: Slants into and secures the A gap.

WEAK END: Slants across the offensive tackle's face into the B gap.

WHIP: Creeps toward the line during cadence and gives the impression that he's rushing from the edge. Contains weakside run and chases strongside run. Spies the near back versus pass.

ASSASSIN: Covers the tight end.

STRONG CORNER: Covers receiver #1 (inside technique).

WEAK CORNER: Covers receiver #1 (inside technique).

STUNT #12

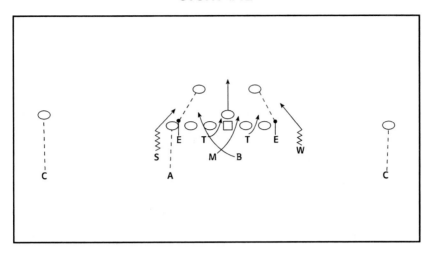

STUNT DESCRIPTION: This is an illusion stunt that gives the offense the *illusion* of an eight-man pass rush.

SECONDARY COVERAGE: Zero coverage. The ends spy the two running backs. Possible variation: assign the outside linebackers to spy and allow the ends to rush.

STUD: Creeps toward the line during cadence and rushes from the edge. Contains strongside run and chases weakside run. Contains the quarterback versus pass.

STRONG END: Plays 7 technique versus run. Spies the near back versus pass.

STRONG TACKLE: Slants across the offensive guard's face into the A gap.

MIKE: Blitzes through the weakside A gap. Mike goes first.

BUCK: Blitzes through the outside shoulder of the offensive guard and secures the strongside B gap. Allows Mike to clear first.

WEAK TACKLE: Slants into and secures the B gap.

WEAK END: Plays 7 technique versus run. Spies the near back versus pass.

WHIP: Creeps toward the line during cadence and rushes from the edge. Contains weakside run and chases strongside run. Contains the quarterback versus pass.

ASSASSIN: Covers the tight end.

STRONG CORNER: Covers receiver #1 (inside technique).

WEAK CORNER: Covers receiver #1 (inside technique).

STUNT #13

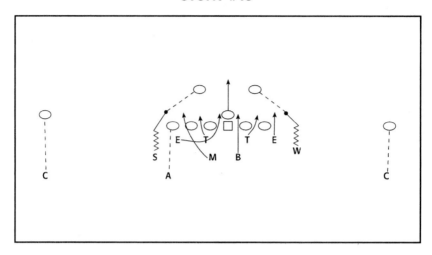

STUNT DESCRIPTION: This is an illusion stunt that gives the offense the *illusion* of an eight-man pass rush.

SECONDARY COVERAGE: Zero coverage. The outside linebackers spy the two running backs. Possible variation: assign Mike and the weak end to spy and allow the outside linebackers to rush.

STUD: Creeps toward the line during cadence and gives the impression that he's rushing from the edge. Contains strongside run and chases weakside run. Spies the near back versus pass.

STRONG END: Loops across the offensive guard's face into the strongside A gap.

STRONG TACKLE: Slants into the B gap.

MIKE: Blitzes through the outside shoulder of the offensive tackle. Secures the C gap versus run and contains the quarterback versus pass.

BUCK: Blitzes through the A gap.

WEAK TACKLE: Slants into and secures the B gap.

WEAK END: Plays 7 technique versus run. Contains the quarterback versus run.

WHIP: Creeps toward the line during cadence and gives the impression that he's rushing from the edge. Contains weakside run and chases strongside run. Spies the near back versus pass.

ASSASSIN: Covers the tight end.

STRONG CORNER: Covers receiver #1 (inside technique).

WEAK CORNER: Covers receiver #1 (inside technique).

STUNT #14

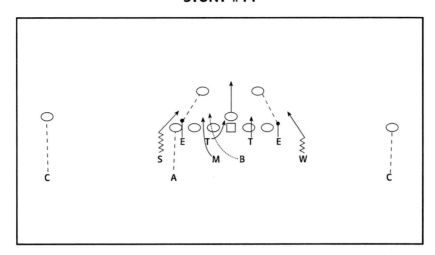

STUNT DESCRIPTION: This is a strongside illusion that develops into a strongside overload versus pass.

SECONDARY COVERAGE: Zero coverage. The ends spy the two running backs. Possible variation: assign the outside linebackers to spy and allow the ends to rush.

STUD: Creeps toward the line during cadence and rushes from the edge. Contains strongside run and chases weakside run. Contains the quarterback versus pass.

STRONG END: Plays 7 technique versus run. Spies the near back versus pass.

STRONG TACKLE: Slants into the A gap.

MIKE: Blitzes through the B gap.

BUCK: Plays base read versus run. Blitzes through the strongside B gap versus pass.

WEAK TACKLE: Plays 3 technique.

WEAK END: Plays 7 technique versus run. Spies the near back versus pass.

WHIP: Creeps toward the line during cadence and rushes from the edge. Contains weakside run and chases strongside run. Contains the quarterback versus pass.

ASSASSIN: Covers the tight end.

STRONG CORNER: Covers receiver #1 (inside technique).

WEAK CORNER: Covers receiver #1 (inside technique).

STUNT #15

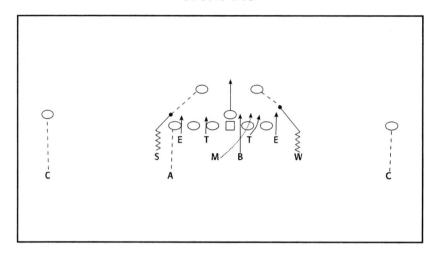

STUNT DESCRIPTION: This is a weakside illusion that develops into a weakside overload versus pass

SECONDARY COVERAGE: Zero coverage. The outside linebackers spy the two running backs. Possible variation: assign the ends to spy and allow the outside linebackers to rush.

STUD: Creeps toward the line during cadence and gives the impression that he's rushing from the edge. Contains strongside run and chases weakside run. Spies the near back versus pass.

STRONG END: Plays 7 technique versus run. Contains the quarterback versus pass.

STRONG TACKLE: Plays 3 technique.

MIKE: Plays base read versus run. Blitzes through the strongside B gap versus pass.

BUCK: Blitzes through the A gap.

WEAK TACKLE: Slants into the B gap.

WEAK END: Plays 7 technique versus run. Contains the quarterback versus pass.

WHIP: Creeps toward the line during cadence and gives the impression that he's rushing from the edge. Contains weakside run and chases strongside run. Spies the near back versus pass.

ASSASSIN: Covers the tight end.

STRONG CORNER: Covers receiver #1 (inside technique).

WEAK CORNER: Covers receiver #1 (inside technique).

STUNT #16

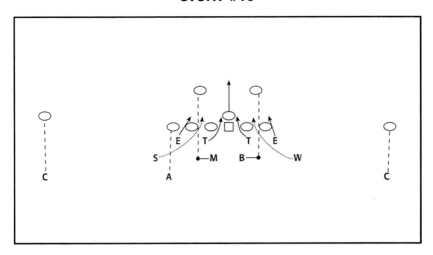

STUNT DESCRIPTION: This is a delayed blitz that provides the defense with a six-man pass rush.

SECONDARY COVERAGE: Zero coverage. Mike and Buck cover the two running backs.

STUD: Plays 8 technique versus run. Blitzes through the B gap versus pass.

STRONG END: Slants through the outside shoulder of the offensive tackle. Secures the C gap and contains the quarterback.

STRONG TACKLE: Slants into the A gap.

MIKE: Shuffles outside at the snap and secures the B gap versus run. Covers the near back versus pass.

BUCK: Shuffles outside at the snap and secures the B gap versus run. Covers the near back versus pass.

WEAK TACKLE: Slants into the A gap.

WEAK END: Slants through the outside shoulder of the offensive tackle. Secures the C gap and contains the quarterback.

WHIP: Plays 8 technique versus run. Blitzes through the B gap versus pass.

ASSASSIN: Covers the tight end.

STRONG CORNER: Covers receiver #1 (inside technique).

WEAK CORNER: Covers receiver #1 (inside technique).

STUNT #17

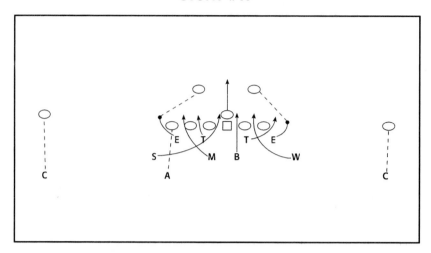

STUNT DESCRIPTION: This is an illusion stunt that gives the *illusion* of an eight-man pass rush.

SECODARY COVERAGE: The ends spy the near back.

STUD: Blitzes through the strongside A gap at the snap.

STRONG END: Slants across the face of the tight end into the D gap. Secures the D gap versus strongside run, chases weakside run, and spies the near back versus pass.

STRONG TACKLE: Slants into the B gap.

MIKE: Blitzes through the outside shoulder of the offensive tackle. Secures the C gap versus run and contains the quarterback versus pass.

BUCK: Blitzes through the A gap.

WEAK TACKLE: Loops across the face of the offensive tackle. Secures the C gap versus run and contains the quarterback versus pass.

WEAK END: Slants outside. Secures the D gap versus weakside run, Chases strongside run and spies the near back versus pass.

WHIP: Lines up in a loose 8 technique and blitzes through the B gap at the snap.

ASSASSIN: Covers the tight end.

STRONG CORNER: Covers receiver #1 (inside technique).

WEAK CORNER: Covers receiver #1 (inside technique).

STUNT #18

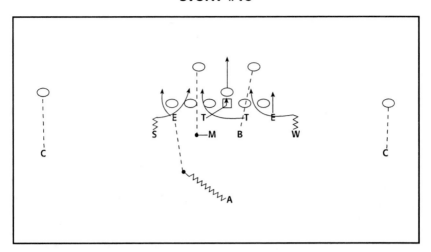

STUNT DESCRIPTION: This is a blitz that provides the defense with a six-man pass rush.

SECONDARY COVERAGE: Zero coverage disguised as cover 1. Mike and Buck cover the two running backs.

STUD: Creeps toward the line and gives the impression that he's rushing from the edge. At the snap, he slants through the outside shoulder of the offensive tackle and secures the C gap.

STRONG END: Slants across the face of the tight end into the D gap. Secures the D gap versus strongside run, and chases weakside run. Contains the quarterback versus pass.

STRONG TACKLE: Slants through the near shoulder of the center and secures the strongside A gap.

MIKE: Plays base technique versus run. Covers the near back versus pass.

BUCK: Scrapes outside and helps with containment versus weakside run. Pursues strongside run from an inside-out position. Covers the near back versus pass.

WEAK TACKLE: Loops across the face of the offensive guard and secures the strongside B gap.

WEAK END: Plays 7 technique versus run. Contains the quarterback versus pass.

WHIP: Creeps toward the line and gives the impression that he's rushing from the edge. At the snap, he slants through the outside shoulder of the offensive tackle and secures the C gap.

ASSASSIN: Covers the tight end.

STRONG CORNER: Covers receiver #1 (inside technique).

WEAK CORNER: Covers receiver #1 (inside technique).

STUNT #19

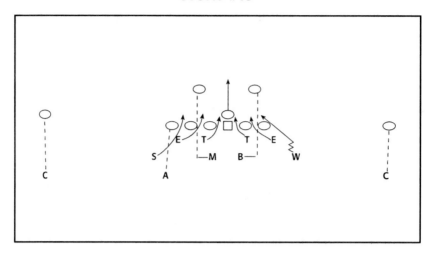

STUNT DESCRIPTION: This is a blitz that provides the defense with a six-man pass rush.

SECONDARY COVERAGE: Zero coverage. Mike and Buck cover the two running backs.

STUD: Blitzes through the C gap at the snap. Secures the C gap and contains the quarterback.

STRONG END: Slants across the face of the offensive tackle and secures the B gap.

STRONG TACKLE: Slants into the A gap.

MIKE: Shuffles laterally at the snap. Scrapes outside and contains strongside run. Pursues weakside run from an inside-out position. Covers the near back versus pass.

BUCK: Shuffles laterally at the snap. Scrapes outside and contains weakside run. Pursues strongside run from an inside-out position. Covers the near back versus pass.

WEAK TACKLE: Slants into the A gap.

WEAK END: Slants across the face of the offensive tackle and secures the B gap.

WHIP: Lines up in a loose 8 technique and blitzes through the outside shoulder of the offensive tackle. Secures the C gap versus run and contains the quarterback versus pass.

ASSASSIN: Covers the tight end.

STRONG CORNER: Covers receiver #1 (inside technique).

WEAK CORNER: Covers receiver #1 (inside technique).

STUNT #20

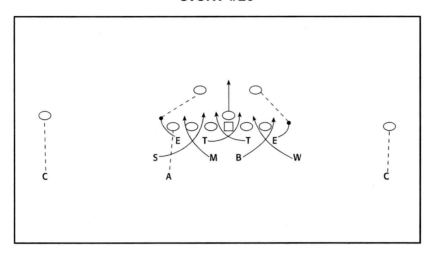

STUNT DESCRIPTION: This is an illusion stunt that gives the *illusion* of an eight-man pass rush.

SECONDARY COVERAGE: Zero coverage. The ends spy the two running backs.

STUD: Blitzes through the B gap at the snap.

STRONG END: Slants across the face of the tight end into the D gap. Secures the D gap versus strongside run, and chases weakside run. Spies the near back versus pass.

STRONG TACKLE: Twists into the weakside A gap. The weak tackle goes first.

MIKE: Blitzes through the outside shoulder of the offensive tackle. Secures the C gap versus run and contains the quarterback versus pass.

BUCK: Blitzes through the outside shoulder of the offensive tackle. Secures the C gap versus run and contains the quarterback versus pass.

WEAK TACKLE: Twists into the strongside A gap. The weak tackle goes first.

WEAK END: Slants outside and secures the D gap versus weakside run, and chases strongside run. Spies the near back versus pass.

WHIP: Lines up in a loose 8 technique and blitzes through the B gap at the snap.

ASSASSIN: Covers the tight end.

STRONG CORNER: Covers receiver #1 (inside technique).

WEAK CORNER: Covers receiver #1 (inside technique).

STUNT #21

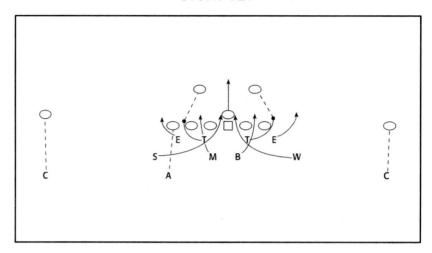

STUNT DESCRIPTION: This is an illusion stunt that gives the *illusion* of an eight-man pass rush.

SECONDARY COVERAGE: Zero coverage. The tackles spy the two running backs. Possible variation: assign the ends to spy and allow the tackles to rush.

STUD: Blitzes through the A gap at the snap.

STRONG END: Slants across the face of the tight end into the D gap. Secures the D gap versus strongside run, and chases weakside run. Contains the quarterback versus pass.

STRONG TACKLE: Slants across the face of the offensive tackle and secures the C gap.

MIKE: Blitzes through the B gap.

BUCK: Blitzes through the B gap.

WEAK TACKLE: Slants across the face of the offensive tackle and secures the C gap.

WEAK END: Slants outside and secures the D gap versus weakside run, chases strongside run. Contains the quarterback versus pass.

WHIP: Lines up in a loose 8 technique and blitzes through the A gap at the snap.

ASSASSIN: Covers the tight end.

STRONG CORNER: Covers receiver #1 (inside technique).

WEAK CORNER: Covers receiver #1 (inside technique).

STUNT #22

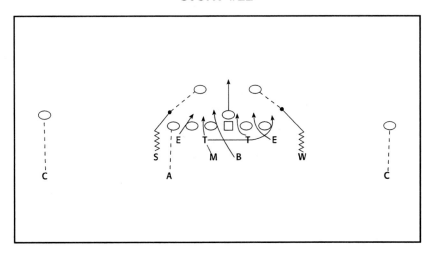

STUNT DESCRIPTION: This is an illusion stunt that gives the *illusion* of an eight-man pass rush.

SECONDARY COVERAGE: Zero coverage. Stud and Whip spy the two running backs.

STUD: Creeps toward the line as though he's going to rush from the edge. Contains strongside run and chases weakside run. Spies the near back versus pass.

STRONG END: Slants through the outside shoulder of the offensive tackle. Secures the C gap and contains the quarterback.

STRONG TACKLE: Loops across the outside shoulder of the offensive tackle. Secures the weakside C gap and contains the quarterback.

MIKE: Blitzes through the outside shoulder of the offensive guard and secures the B gap.

BUCK: Blitzes through the inside shoulder of the offensive guard and secures the strongside A gap.

WEAK TACKLE: Slants across the face of the offensive guard and secures the A gap.

WEAK END: Slants across the face of the offensive tackle and secures the B gap.

WHIP: Lines up in a loose 8 technique. Creeps toward the line as though he's going to rush from the edge. Contains strongside run and chases weakside run. Spies the near back versus pass.

ASSASSIN: Covers the tight end.

STRONG CORNER: Covers receiver #1 (inside technique).

WEAK CORNER: Covers receiver #1 (inside technique).

STUNT #23

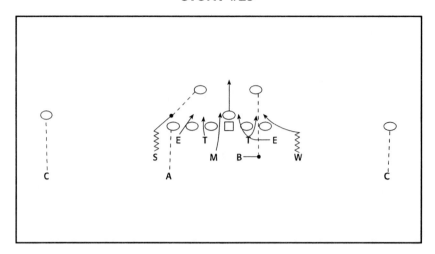

STUNT DESCRIPTION: This is an illusion stunt that gives the *illusion* of a seven-man pass rush.

SECONDARY COVERAGE: Zero coverage. Stud and Buck cover the two running backs.

STUD: Creeps toward the line as though he's going to rush from the edge. Contains strongside run and chases weakside run. Spies the near back versus pass.

STRONG END: Slants through the outside shoulder of the offensive tackle. Secures the C gap and contains the quarterback.

STRONG TACKLE: Slants into the B gap.

MIKE: Blitzes through the A gap.

BUCK: Shuffles slightly to the outside at the snap. Scrapes outside and contains versus weakside run. Pursues strongside run from an inside-out position. Covers the near back versus pass.

WEAK TACKLE: Slants into the B gap.

WEAK END: Loops across the face of the offensive guard and secures the weakside A gap.

WHIP: Lines up in a loose 8 technique. Creeps toward the line during cadence and attacks the offensive tackle's outside shoulder. Secures the C gap and contains the quarterback.

ASSASSIN: Covers the tight end.

STRONG CORNER: Covers receiver #1 (inside technique).

WEAK CORNER: Covers receiver #1 (inside technique).

STUNT #24

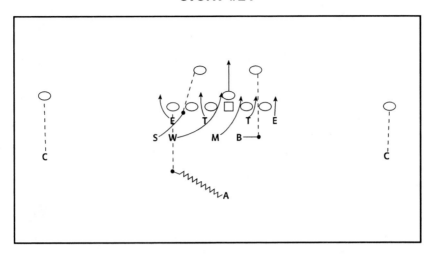

STUNT DESCRIPTION: This is an illusion stunt that gives the *illusion* of a seven-man pass rush.

SECONDARY COVERAGE: Zero coverage. Stud and Buck cover the two running backs.

STUD: Stunts toward the C gap. Secures the C gap versus run and spies the near back versus pass.

STRONG END: Slants across the face of the tight end. Contains the quarterback and strongside run. Chases weakside run.

STRONG TACKLE: Slants into the B gap.

MIKE: Blitzes through the weakside A gap.

BUCK: Shuffles slightly to the outside at the snap. Scrapes outside and contains versus weakside run. Pursues strongside run from an inside-out position. Covers the near back versus pass.

WEAK TACKLE: Slants into the B gap.

WEAK END: Plays 7 technique versus run. Contains the quarterback versus pass.

WHIP: Lines up five yards deep, directly behind the strong end. Blitzes through the strongside A gap at the snap.

ASSASSIN: Covers the tight end. Disguises his assignment as though he's playing cover 1.

STRONG CORNER: Covers receiver #1 (inside technique).

WEAK CORNER: Covers receiver #1 (inside technique).

STUNT #25

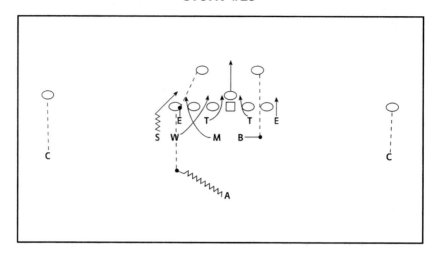

STUNT DESCRIPTION: This is an overload blitz that gives the defense four strongside pass rushers.

SECONDARY COVERAGE: Zero coverage. The strong end and Buck cover the two running backs.

STUD: Creeps toward the line during cadence and rushes from the edge. Contains the quarterback and strongside run. Chases weakside run.

STRONG END: Plays 7 technique versus run. Spies the near back versus pass.

STRONG TACKLE: Slants across the offensive guard's face into the A gap.

MIKE: Blitzes through the outside shoulder of the offensive tackle and secures the C gap.

BUCK: Shuffles slightly to the outside at the snap. Scrapes outside and contains versus weakside run. Pursues strongside run from an inside-out position. Covers the near back versus pass.

WEAK TACKLE: Slants across the offensive guard's face into the A gap.

WEAK END: Plays 7 technique versus run. Contains the quarterback versus pass.

WHIP: Lines up five yards deep directly behind the strong end. Blitzes through the strongside B gap at the snap.

ASSASSIN: Covers the tight end. Disguises his assignment as though he's playing cover 1.

STRONG CORNER: Covers receiver #1 (inside technique).

WEAK CORNER: Covers receiver #1 (inside technique).

STUNT #26

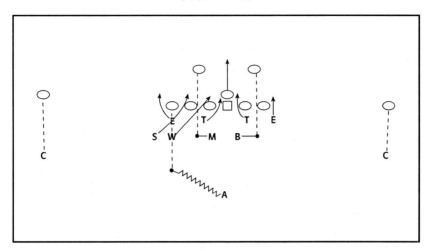

STUNT DESCRIPTION: This is an overload blitz that gives the defense four strongside pass rushers.

SECONDARY COVERAGE: Zero coverage. Mike and Buck cover the two running backs.

STUD: Blitzes through the outside shoulder of the offensive tackle and secures the C gap.

STRONG END: Slants across the face of the tight end. Contains the quarterback and strongside run. Chases weakside run.

STRONG TACKLE: Slants across the offensive guard's face into the A gap.

MIKE: Shuffles slightly to the outside at the snap. Pursues both strongside and weakside run from an inside-out position. Covers the near back versus pass.

BUCK: Shuffles slightly to the outside at the snap. Scrapes outside and contains versus weakside run. Pursues strongside run from an inside-out position. Covers the near back versus pass.

WEAK TACKLE: Slants across the offensive guard's face into the A gap.

WEAK END: Plays 7 technique versus run. Contains the quarterback versus pass.

WHIP: Lines up five yards deep directly behind the strong end. Blitzes through the strongside B gap at the snap.

ASSASSIN: Covers the tight end. Disguises his assignment as though he's playing cover 1.

STRONG CORNER: Covers receiver #1 (inside technique).

WEAK CORNER: Covers receiver #1 (inside technique).

STUNT #27

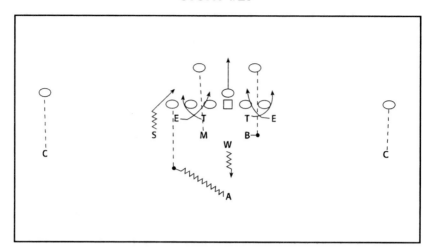

STUNT DESCRIPTION: This is a dog with a double line twist.

SECONDARY COVERAGE: Zero coverage disguised as cover 1 with Whip acting as a "robber." Buck and Mike cover the two running backs.

STUD: Creeps toward the line during cadence and rushes from the edge. Contains the quarterback and strongside run. Chases weakside run.

STRONG END: Loops through the outside shoulder of the offensive guard and secures the B gap. The tackle goes first. The strong end makes his first step parallel to the line with his right foot.

STRONG TACKLE: Slants across the face of the offensive tackle and secures the C gap.

MIKE: Pursues strongside and weakside run from an inside-out position. Covers the near back versus pass.

BUCK: Shuffles slightly to the outside at the snap. Scrapes outside and contains versus weakside run. Pursues strongside run from an inside-out position. Covers the near back versus pass.

WEAK TACKLE: Slants across the face of the offensive tackle and secures the C gap. Contains the quarterback versus pass.

WEAK END: Loops through the outside shoulder of the offensive guard and secures the B gap. The tackle goes first. The weak end makes his first step parallel to the line with his right foot.

WHIP: Lines up in the "C" position. He is responsible for the cutback versus run. He is the "robber" versus pass.

ASSASSIN: Covers the tight end. Disguises his assignment as though he's playing cover 1.

STRONG CORNER: Covers receiver #1 (inside technique).

WEAK CORNER: Covers receiver #1 (inside technique).

STUNT #28

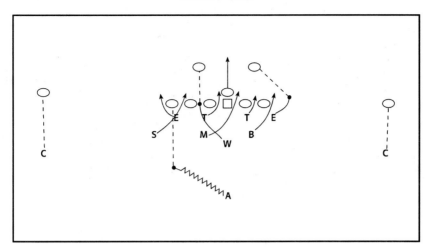

STUNT DESCRIPTION: This is an illusion stunt that gives the *illusion* of an eight-man pass rush.

SECONDARY COVERAGE: Zero coverage disguised as cover 1. Whip and the weak end cover the two running backs.

STUD: Blitzes through the C gap.

STRONG END: Slants across the face of the tight end and contains the quarterback and strongside run. Chases weakside run.

STRONG TACKLE: Slants across the face of the offensive guard and secures the A gap.

MIKE: Blitzes through the weakside A gap.

BUCK: Blitzes through the outside shoulder of the offensive tackle. Secures the C gap and contains the quarterback.

WEAK TACKLE: Slants into the B gap.

WEAK END: Slants outside. Contains weakside run and chases strongside run. Spies the near back versus pass.

WHIP: Lines up in the "C" position. Stunts toward the strongside B gap. Secures the B gap versus run and spies the near back versus pass.

ASSASSIN: Covers the tight end. Disguises his assignment as though he's playing cover 1.

STRONG CORNER: Covers receiver #1 (inside technique).

WEAK CORNER: Covers receiver #1 (inside technique).

STUNT #29

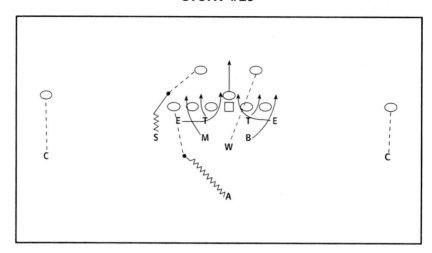

STUNT DESCRIPTION: This is an illusion stunt that gives the *illusion* of a seven-man pass rush.

SECONDARY COVERAGE: Zero coverage disguised as cover 1. Whip and Stud cover the two running backs.

STUD: Creeps toward the line during cadence. Contains strongside run and chases weakside run. Spies the near back versus pass.

STRONG END: Loops through the inside shoulder of the offensive guard and secures the A gap.

STRONG TACKLE: Slants into the B gap.

MIKE: Blitzes through the outside shoulder of the offensive tackle. Secures the C gap and contains the quarterback.

BUCK: Blitzes through the outside shoulder of the offensive tackle. Secures the C gap and contains the quarterback.

WEAK TACKLE: Slants into the B gap.

WEAK END: Loops through the inside shoulder of the offensive guard and secures the A gap.

WHIP: Lines up in the "C" position. Responsible for cutback versus strongside run. Scrapes outside and contains versus weakside run. Covers the near back versus pass.

ASSASSIN: Covers the tight end. Disguises his assignment as though he's playing cover 1.

STRONG CORNER: Covers receiver #1 (inside technique).

WEAK CORNER: Covers receiver #1 (inside technique).

STUNT #30

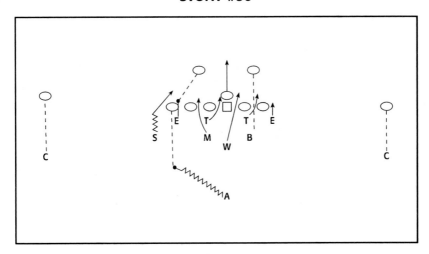

STUNT DESCRIPTION: This is an illusion stunt that gives the *illusion* of a seven-man pass rush.

SECONDARY COVERAGE: Zero coverage disguised as cover 1. Whip and Stud cover the two running backs.

STUD: Creeps toward the line during cadence and rushes from the edge. Contains the quarterback and strongside run. Chases weakside run.

STRONG END: Plays 7 technique versus run. Spies the near back versus pass.

STRONG TACKLE: Slants across the offensive guard's face into the A gap.

MIKE: Blitzes through the B gap.

BUCK: Scrapes outside and contains versus weakside run. Responsible for cutback versus strongside run. Covers the near back versus pass.

WEAK TACKLE: Slants into the B gap.

WEAK END: Plays 7 technique versus run. Contains the quarterback versus pass.

WHIP: Lines up in the "C" position and blitzes through the weakside A gap at the snap.

ASSASSIN: Covers the tight end. Disguises his assignment as though he's playing cover 1.

STRONG CORNER: Covers receiver #1 (inside technique).

WEAK CORNER: Covers receiver #1 (inside technique).

STUNT #31

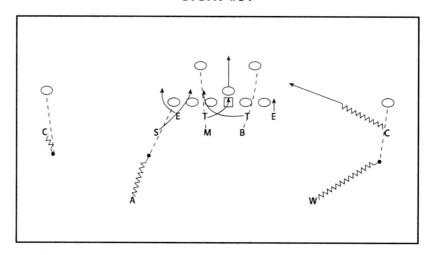

STUNT DESCRIPTION: This is a weak cornerback blitz.

SECONDARY COVERAGE: Zero coverage disguised as cover 2. Mike and Buck cover the two running backs.

STUD: Blitzes through the outside shoulder of the offensive tackle and secures the C gap.

STRONG END: Slants across the face of the tight end. Contains the quarterback and strongside run. Chases weakside run.

STRONG TACKLE: Slants across the offensive guard's face into the near shoulder of the center. Secures the strongside A gap.

MIKE: Pursues strongside and weakside run from an inside-out position. Covers the near back versus pass.

BUCK: Pursues strongside and weakside run from an inside-out position. Covers the near back versus pass.

WEAK TACKLE: Loops across the face of the offensive guard and secures the strongside B gap.

WEAK END: Plays 7 technique.

WHIP: Lines up as though he's playing cover 2. During cadence, he moves to a position that enables him to cover the split end (inside technique).

ASSASSIN: Covers the tight end. Disguises his assignment as though he's playing cover 2.

STRONG CORNER: Covers receiver #1 (inside technique). Disguises his assignment as though he's playing cover 2.

WEAK CORNER: Disguises his assignment as cover 2. During cadence, he slowly creeps inside and blitzes from the edge. Contains the quarterback and weakside run. Chases strongside run.

STUNT #32

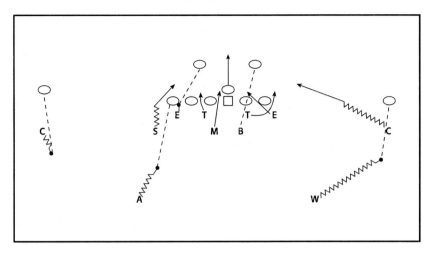

STUNT DESCRIPTION: This is a weak cornerback blitz that gives the illusion of a seven-man pass rush.

SECONDARY COVERAGE: Zero coverage disguised as cover 2. The strong end and Buck cover the two running backs.

STUD: Slowly creeps toward the line during cadence. Contains the quarterback and strongside run. Chases weakside run.

STRONG END: Plays 7 technique versus run. Spies the near back versus pass.

STRONG TACKLE: Slants into the B gap.

MIKE: Blitzes through the A gap.

BUCK: Pursues strongside and weakside run from an inside-out position. Covers the near back versus pass.

WEAK TACKLE: Loops across the face of the offensive tackle and secures the C gap. The end goes first.

WEAK END: Slants into the B gap.

WHIP: Lines up as though he's playing cover 2. During cadence, he moves to a position that enables him to cover the split end (inside technique).

ASSASSIN: Covers the tight end. Disguises his assignment as though he's playing cover 2.

STRONG CORNER: Covers receiver #1 (inside technique). Disguises his assignment as though he's playing cover 2.

WEAK CORNER: Disguises his assignment as cover 2. During cadence, he slowly creeps inside and blitzes from the edge. Contains the quarterback and weakside run. Chases strongside run.

STUNT #33

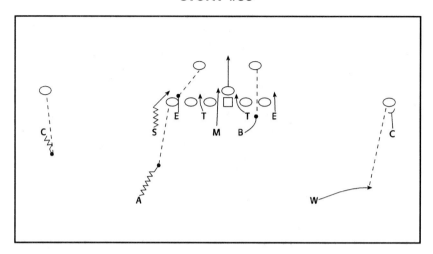

STUNT DESCRIPTION: This dog provides double coverage on the split end.

SECONDARY COVERAGE: Zero coverage disguised as cover 2. The strong end and Buck cover the two running backs.

STUD: Slowly creeps toward the line during cadence. Contains the quarterback and strongside run. Chases weakside run.

STRONG END: Plays 7 technique versus run. Spies the near back versus pass.

STRONG TACKLE: Slants into the B gap.

MIKE: Blitzes through the A gap.

BUCK: Stunts toward the B gap. Secures the B gap versus run and spies the near back versus pass.

WEAK TACKLE: Slants across the offensive guard's face into the A gap.

WEAK END: Plays 7 technique versus run. Contains the quarterback versus pass.

WHIP: Lines up as though he's playing cover 2. During cadence, he moves to a position that enables him to double cover the split end. He is responsible for deep patterns.

ASSASSIN: Covers the tight end. Disguises his assignment as though he's playing cover 2.

STRONG CORNER: Covers receiver #1 (inside technique). Disguises his assignment as though he's playing cover 2.

WEAK CORNER: Disguises his assignment as cover 2. Double covers the split end with Whip. Aggressively funnels the split end inside.

STUNT #34

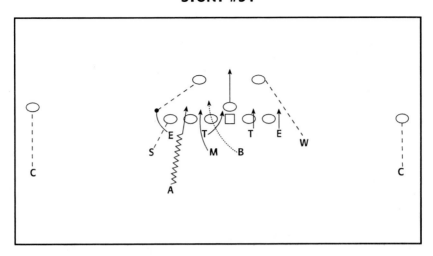

STUNT DESCRIPTION: This Assassin/delayed-linebacker blitz provides the defense with an overload strongside pass rush.

SECONDARY COVERAGE: A variation of zero coverage. The strong end and Buck cover the two running backs, and Stud covers the tight end.

STUD: Covers the tight end.

STRONG END: Slants across the tight end's face into the D gap. Contains strongside run and chases weakside run. Spies the near back versus pass.

STRONG TACKLE: Slants into the A gap.

MIKE: Blitzes through the B gap.

BUCK: Plays base technique versus run. Blitzes through the strongside B gap versus pass.

WEAK TACKLE: Plays 3 technique.

WEAK END: Plays 7 technique versus run. Contains the quarterback versus pass.

WHIP: Plays 8 technique versus run. Covers the near back versus pass.

ASSASSIN: Blitzes through the C gap. Secures the C gap versus run and contains the quarterback.

STRONG CORNER: Covers receiver #1 (inside technique).

WEAK CORNER: Covers receiver #1 (inside technique).

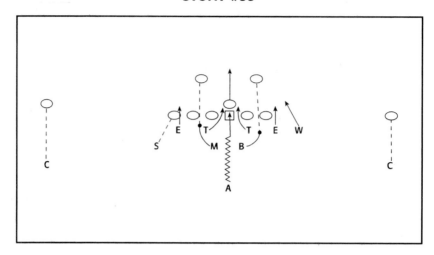

STUNT DESCRIPTION: This Assassin blitz provides the defense with the *illusion* of an eight-man pass rush.

SECONDARY COVERAGE: A variation of zero coverage. Mike and Buck spy the two running backs, and Stud covers the tight end.

STUD: Covers the tight end.

STRONG END: Plays 7 technique versus run. Contains the quarterback versus pass.

STRONG TACKLE: Slants into the A gap.

MIKE: Stunts toward the B gap. Secures the B gap versus run and spies the near back versus pass.

BUCK: Stunts toward the B gap. Secures the B gap versus run and spies the near back versus pass.

WEAK TACKLE: Slants into the A gap.

WEAK END: Plays 7 technique.

WHIP: Rushes from the edge. Contains the quarterback and weakside run. Chases strongside run.

ASSASSIN: Disguises his assignment as though he's playing cover 1. Creeps toward the line during cadence and blitzes through the face of the center as the ball is being snapped.

STRONG CORNER: Covers receiver #1 (inside technique).

WEAK CORNER: Covers receiver #1 (inside technique).

STUNT #36

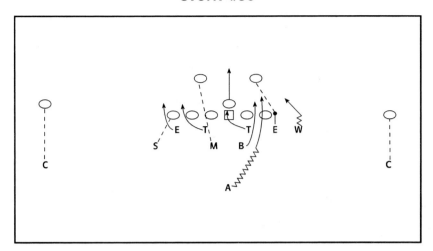

STUNT DESCRIPTION: This stunt is both a twin stunt and an Assassin blitz. It provides the defense with the illusion of an eight-man pass rush.

SECONDARY COVERAGE: A variation of zero coverage. Mike and the weak end cover the two running backs, and Stud covers the tight end.

STUD: Covers the tight end.

STRONG END: Slants across the face of the tight end. Contains the quarterback and strongside run. Chases weakside run.

STRONG TACKLE: Slants across the face of the offensive tackle and secures the C gap.

MIKE: Fills the B gap versus strongside run. Pursues weakside run from an inside-out position. Covers the near back versus pass.

BUCK: Blitzes through the outside shoulder of the offensive guard.

WEAK TACKLE: Slants to the head of the center and controls both A gaps.

WEAK END: Plays 7 technique versus run. Spies the near back versus pass.

WHIP: Rushes from the edge. Contains the quarterback and weakside run. Chases strongside run.

ASSASSIN: Disguises his assignment as though he's playing cover 1. Creeps toward the line during cadence and blitzes through the inside shoulder of the offensive tackle as the ball is being snapped.

STRONG CORNER: Covers receiver #1 (inside technique).

WEAK CORNER: Covers receiver #1 (inside technique).

STUNT #37

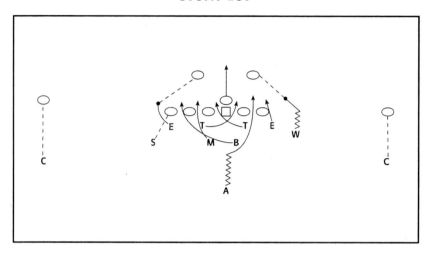

STUNT DESCRIPTION: This Assassin blitz provides the defense with the *illusion* of an eight-man pass rush and causes a multitude of blocking problems for the offense.

SECONDARY COVERAGE: A variation of zero coverage. The strong end and Whip cover the two running backs, and Stud covers the tight end.

STUD: Covers the tight end.

STRONG END: Slants across the face of the tight end. Contains strongside run and chases weakside run. Spies the near back versus pass.

STRONG TACKLE: Slants across the face of the center and secures the weakside A gap. Because the weak tackle goes first, the strong tackle makes his first step with his right foot parallel to the line.

MIKE: Blitzes through the B gap.

BUCK: Blitzes through the outside shoulder of the offensive tackle. Secures the strongside C gap and contains the quarterback.

WEAK TACKLE: Slants into the strongside A gap. Weak tackle goes first.

WEAK END: Plays 7 technique versus run. Contains the quarterback versus pass.

WHIP: Rushes from the edge. Contains weakside run and chases strongside run. Spies the near back versus pass.

ASSASSIN: Disguises his assignment as though he's playing cover 1. Creeps toward the line during cadence and blitzes through the weakside B gap as the ball is being snapped.

STRONG CORNER: Covers receiver #1 (inside technique).

WEAK CORNER: Covers receiver #1 (inside technique).

STUNT #38

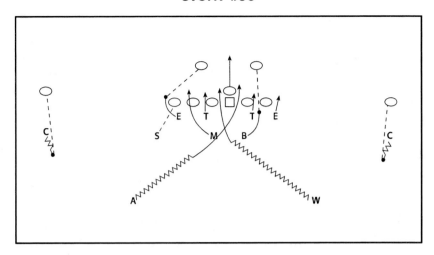

STUNT DESCRIPTION: This double-safety blitz gives the offense the *illusion* that the defense is "bringing the house." This is a good stunt versus pass but vulnerable against weakside run.

SECONDARY COVERAGE: A variation of zero coverage disguised as cover 2. The strong end and Buck cover the two running backs, and Stud covers the tight end.

STUD: Covers the tight end.

STRONG END: Slants across the face of the tight end. Contains strongside run and chases weakside run. Spies the near back versus pass.

STRONG TACKLE: Plays 3 technique.

MIKE: Blitzes through the outside shoulder of the offensive tackle and secures the C gap. Contains the quarterback versus pass.

BUCK: Stunts toward the B gap. Secures the B gap versus run. Spies the near back versus pass.

WEAK TACKLE: Plays 3 technique.

WEAK END: Plays 7 technique versus run. Contains the quarterback versus pass.

WHIP: Disguises his assignment as though he's playing cover 2. Creeps toward the line during cadence and blitzes through the strongside A gap.

ASSASSIN: Disguises his assignment as though he's playing cover 2. Creeps toward the line during cadence and blitzes through the weakside A gap.

STRONG CORNER: Covers receiver #1 (inside technique). Disguises his assignment as cover 2.

WEAK CORNER: Covers receiver #1 (inside technique). Disguises his assignment as cover 2.

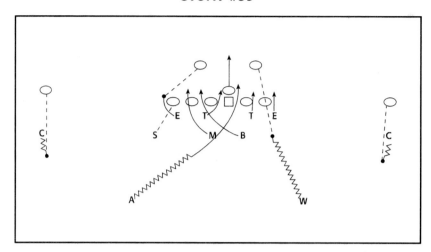

STUNT DESCRIPTION: This fake double-safety blitz gives the offense the *illusion* that the defense is "bringing the house."

SECONDARY COVERAGE: A variation of zero coverage disguised as cover 2. The strong end and Whip cover the two running backs, and Stud covers the tight end.

STUD: Covers the tight end.

STRONG END: Slants across the face of the tight end. Contains strongside run and chases weakside run. Spies the near back versus pass.

STRONG TACKLE: Slants across the face of the offensive guard into the A gap.

MIKE: Blitzes through the outside shoulder of the offensive tackle and secures the C gap. Contains the quarterback versus pass.

BUCK: Blitzes through the outside shoulder of the offensive guard and secures the strongside B gap.

WEAK TACKLE: Plays 3 technique.

WEAK END: Plays 7 technique versus run. Contains the quarterback versus pass.

WHIP: Disguises his assignment as though he's playing cover 2. Creeps toward the line during cadence and threatens to blitz through the weakside B gap. Contains weakside run and spies the near back.

ASSASSIN: Disguises his assignment as though he's playing cover 2. Creeps toward the line during cadence and blitzes through the weakside A gap.

STRONG CORNER: Covers receiver #1 (inside technique). Disguises his assignment as cover 2.

WEAK CORNER: Covers receiver #1 (inside technique). Disguises his assignment as cover 2.

STUNT #40

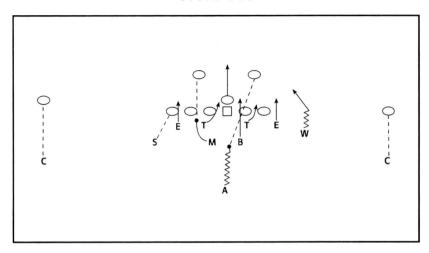

STUNT DESCRIPTION: This fake Assassin blitz provides the defense with a weakside overload pass rush.

SECONDARY COVERAGE: A variation of zero coverage. Assassin and Mike cover the two running backs, and Stud covers the tight end.

STUD: Covers the tight end.

STRONG END: Plays 7 technique versus run. Contains the quarterback versus pass.

STRONG TACKLE: Slants across the face of the offensive guard into the A gap.

MIKE: Stunts toward the B gap. Secures the B gap versus run and spies the near back versus pass.

BUCK: Blitzes through the inside shoulder of the offensive guard and secures the A gap.

WEAK TACKLE: Slants into the B gap.

WEAK END: Plays 7 technique.

WHIP: Rushes from the edge. Contains the quarterback and weakside run. Chases strongside run.

ASSASSIN: Disguises his assignment as though he's playing cover 1. Creeps toward the line during cadence and gives the impression that he's going to blitz through the one of the A gaps. Fills the alleys versus run and spies the weakside halfback versus pass.

STRONG CORNER: Covers receiver #1 (inside technique).

WEAK CORNER: Covers receiver #1 (inside technique).

STUNT #41

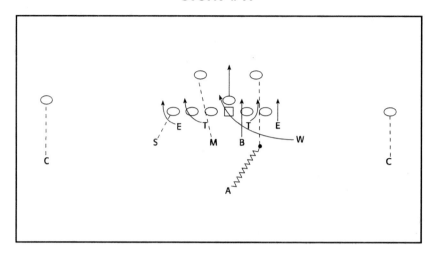

STUNT DESCRIPTION: This fake Assassin blitz provides the defense with a six-man pass rush.

SECONDARY COVERAGE: A variation of zero coverage. The Assassin and Mike cover the two running backs, and Stud covers the tight end.

STUD: Covers the tight end.

STRONG END: Slants across the face of the tight end into the D gap. Contains the quarterback and strongside run. Chases weakside run.

STRONG TACKLE: Slants across the face of the offensive tackle and secures the C gap.

MIKE: Fills the B gap versus strongside run. Pursues weakside run from an inside-out position. Covers the near back versus pass.

BUCK: Blitzes through the inside shoulder of the offensive guard and secures the A gap.

WEAK TACKLE: Slants into the B gap.

WEAK END: Plays 7 technique versus run. Contains the quarterback versus pass.

WHIP: Blitzes through the strongside A gap.

ASSASSIN: Disguises his assignment as though he's playing cover 1. Creeps toward the line during cadence and gives the impression that he's blitzing weakside. Contains weakside run and covers the near back versus pass.

STRONG CORNER: Covers receiver #1 (inside technique).

WEAK CORNER: Covers receiver #1 (inside technique).

STUNT #42

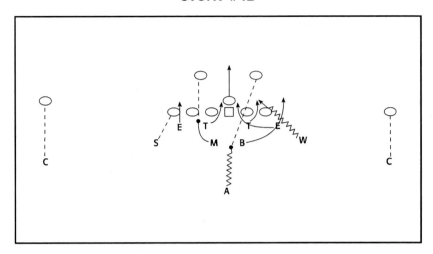

STUNT DESCRIPTION: This fake Assassin blitz provides the defense with a weakside overload pass rush.

SECONDARY COVERAGE: A variation of zero coverage. Assassin and Mike cover the two running backs, and Stud covers the tight end.

STUD: Covers the tight end.

STRONG END: Plays 7 technique versus run. Contains the quarterback versus pass.

STRONG TACKLE: Slants across the face of the offensive guard into the A gap.

MIKE: Stunts toward the B gap. Secures the B gap versus run and spies the near back versus pass.

BUCK: Blitzes into the D gap. Contains the quarterback and strongside run. Chases weakside run.

WEAK TACKLE: Slants into the B gap.

WEAK END: Loops across the face of the offensive guard into the weakside A gap.

WHIP: Creeps toward the line during cadence. Blitzes through the outside shoulder of the offensive tackle and secures the C gap.

ASSASSIN: Disguises his assignment as though he's playing cover 1. Creeps toward the line during cadence and gives the impression that he's going to blitz through one of the A gaps. Fills the alleys versus run and spies the weakside halfback versus pass.

STRONG CORNER: Covers receiver #1 (inside technique).

WEAK CORNER: Covers receiver #1 (inside technique).

STUNT #43

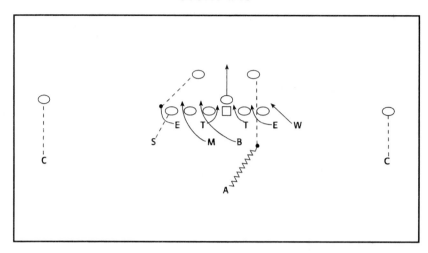

STUNT DESCRIPTION: This fake Assassin blitz gives the *illusion* of a seven-man pass rush.

SECONDARY COVERAGE: A variation of zero coverage. The Assassin and strong end cover the two running backs, and Stud covers the tight end.

STUD: Covers the tight end.

STRONG END: Slants across the face of the tight end into the D gap. Contains strongside run and chases weakside run. Spies the near back versus pass.

STRONG TACKLE: Slants across the face of the offensive guard and secures the A gap.

MIKE: Stunts through the outside shoulder of the offensive tackle. Secures the C gap versus run and contains the quarterback versus pass.

BUCK: Blitzes through the outside shoulder of the offensive guard and secures the strongside B gap.

WEAK TACKLE: Slants into the A gap.

WEAK END: Slants across the face of the offensive tackle into the B gap.

WHIP: Blitzes through the outside shoulder of the offensive tackle. Secures the C gap and contains the quarterback.

ASSASSIN: Disguises his assignment as though he's playing cover 1. Creeps toward the line during cadence and gives the impression that he's blitzing weakside. Contains weakside run and covers the near back versus pass.

STRONG CORNER: Covers receiver #1 (inside technique).

WEAK CORNER: Covers receiver #1 (inside technique).

STUNT #44

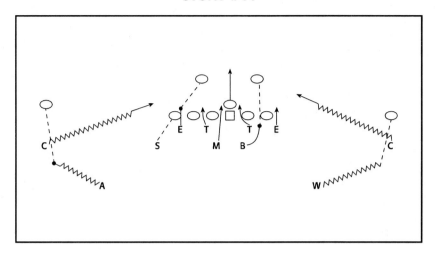

STUNT DESCRIPTION: This is a double-cornerback blitz that gives the *illusion* of an eight-man pass rush.

SECONDARY COVERAGE: A variation of zero coverage disguised as cover 2. The strong end and Buck cover the two running backs. Stud covers the tight end.

STUD: Covers the tight end.

STRONG END: Plays 7 technique versus run. Spies the near back versus pass.

STRONG TACKLE: Slants into the B gap.

MIKE: Blitzes through the A gap.

BUCK: Stunts toward the B gap. Controls the B gap versus run, and spies the near back versus pass.

WEAK TACKLE: Slants into the A gap.

WEAK END: Plays 7 technique.

WHIP: Lines up as though he's playing cover 2. During cadence, moves to a position that enables him to cover the split end (inside technique).

ASSASSIN: Lines up as though he's playing cover 2. During cadence, moves to a position that enables him to cover the flanker (inside technique).

STRONG CORNER: Disguises his assignment as cover 2. During cadence, slowly creeps inside and blitzes from the edge. Contains the quarterback and strongside run. Chases weakside run.

WEAK CORNER: Disguises his assignment as cover 2. During cadence, slowly creeps inside and blitzes from the edge. Contains the quarterback and weakside run. Chases strongside run.

STUNT #45

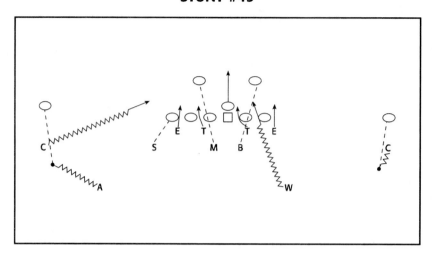

STUNT DESCRIPTION: This is a strong cornerback/Whip blitz that gives the defense a six-man pass rush.

SECONDARY COVERAGE: A variation of zero coverage disguised as cover 2. Mike and Buck cover the two running backs. Stud covers the tight end.

STUD: Covers the tight end.

STRONG END: Plays 7 technique.

STRONG TACKLE: Slants into the B gap.

MIKE: Plays base technique versus run. Covers the near back versus pass.

BUCK: Scrapes outside and contains versus weakside run. Pursues strongside run from an inside-out position. Covers the near back versus pass.

WEAK TACKLE: Slants into the A gap.

WEAK END: Plays 7 technique versus run. Contains the quarterback versus pass.

WHIP: Lines up as though he's playing cover 2. He moves toward the line during cadence, and blitzes through the weakside B gap at the snap.

ASSASSIN: Lines up as though he's playing cover 2. During cadence, moves to a position that enables him to cover the flanker (inside technique).

STRONG CORNER: Disguises his assignment as cover 2. During cadence, slowly creeps inside and blitzes from the edge. Contains the quarterback and strongside run. Chases weakside run.

WEAK CORNER: Covers receiver #1 (inside technique). Disguises his assignment as cover 2.

STUNT #46

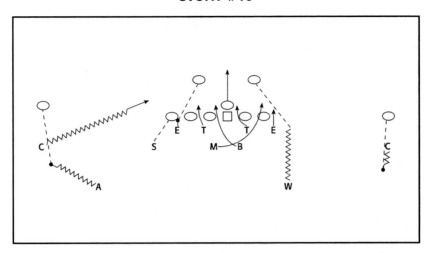

STUNT DESCRIPTION: This is a strong cornerback blitz that gives the defense a six-man pass rush.

SECONDARY COVERAGE: A variation of zero coverage disguised as cover 2. The strong end and Whip cover the two running backs. Stud covers the tight end.

STUD: Covers the tight end.

STRONG END: Plays 7 technique versus run. Spies the near back versus pass.

STRONG TACKLE: Slants into the B gap.

MIKE: Blitzes through the inside shoulder of the offensive tackle and controls the weakside B gap.

BUCK: Blitzes through the strongside A gap.

WEAK TACKLE: Slants into the A gap.

WEAK END: Plays 7 technique versus run. Contains the quarterback versus pass.

WHIP: Lines up as though he's playing cover 2. Moves toward the line during cadence and gives the impression that he's going to rush from the edge. Contains weakside run and chases strongside run. Spies the near back versus pass.

ASSASSIN: Lines up as though he's playing cover 2. During cadence, moves to a position that enables him to cover the flanker (inside technique).

STRONG CORNER: Disguises his assignment as cover 2. During cadence, slowly creeps inside and blitzes from the edge. Contains the quarterback and strongside run. Chases weakside run.

WEAK CORNER: Covers receiver #1 (inside technique). Disguises his assignment as cover 2.

STUNT #47

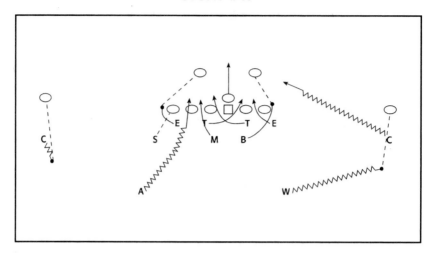

STUNT DESCRIPTION: This cornerback/Assassin blitz gives the *illusion* of an eight-man pass rush.

SECONDARY COVERAGE: A variation of zero coverage disguised as cover 2. The strong end and Buck cover the two running backs. Stud covers the tight end.

STUD: Covers the tight end.

STRONG END: Slants across the face of the tight end. Secures the D gap versus run and spies the near back versus pass.

STRONG TACKLE: Slants into the weakside A gap. Strong tackle goes first.

MIKE: Blitzes through the B gap.

BUCK: Stunts toward the C gap. Controls the C gap versus run and spies the near back versus pass.

WEAK TACKLE: Slants into the strongside A gap. Because the strong tackle goes first, the weak tackle makes his first step parallel to the line with his left foot.

WEAK END: Slants across the face of the offensive tackle into the B gap.

WHIP: Lines up as though he's playing cover 2. During cadence, moves to a position that enables him to cover the split end (inside technique).

ASSASSIN: Lines up as though he's playing cover 2. During cadence, moves toward the line and blitzes through the C gap.

STRONG CORNER: Covers receiver #1 (inside technique). Disguises his assignment as cover 2.

WEAK CORNER: Disguises his assignment as cover 2. During cadence, slowly creeps inside and blitzes from the edge. Contains the quarterback and weakside run. Chases strongside run.

CHAPTER 6

COVER 1 STUNTS

Cover 1 is a man-to-man coverage with either the Assassin or Whip free. One strength of this coverage is that there is always a free safety keying the ball, playing center field, and backing up the other three defensive backs and the seven defenders in the box. Another strength is that since it is a man-to-man coverage, the offense cannot use high-low zones to attack seams. A third strength is that this coverage is easily disguised, which inhibits a quarterback's pre-snap read.

Although it is not as risky as zero coverage, cover 1 does not exert as much pressure on the offense as zero coverage. This weakness can be somewhat offset by incorporating the tactic of *illusion* into its stunt package. Banjo and gumbo are two very important *illusion* tactics that will be implemented in this coverage.

Banjo

As noted in Chapter 1, whenever banjo is employed, three defenders drop into an area (Abel, Baker, and Charlie) and share the joint responsibility of covering the tight end and the two running backs. Each defender is responsible for covering any of the three named receivers who enter his area. Figures 6-1a through 6-1d show how this concept functions against four common pass patterns frequently used to attack it. In the illustration, the Stud drops Abel banjo; Mike drops Baker banjo; and Buck drops Charlie banjo.

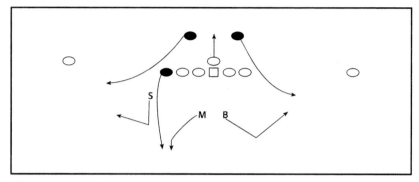

Figure 6-1a

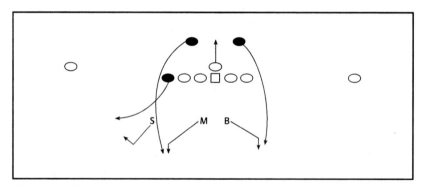

Figure 6-1b

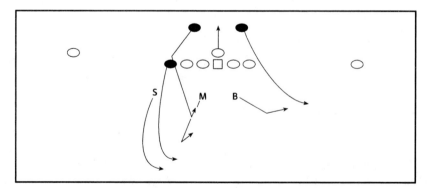

Figure 6-1c

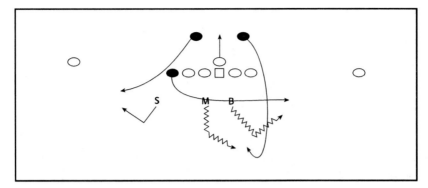

Figure 6-1d

Gumbo

Gumbo is a much simpler concept for defenders to master because only two defenders are being asked to inside-out-combo cover two receivers (the tight end and strongside halfback). Figures 6-2a through 6-2d illustrate how gumbo functions versus four common pass patterns frequently used to attack it. In the illustration, Stud drops Abel gumbo, and Mike drops Baker gumbo.

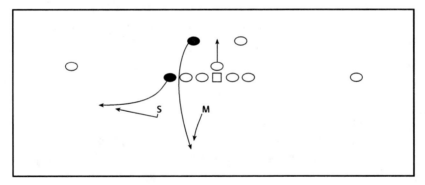

Figure 6-2a

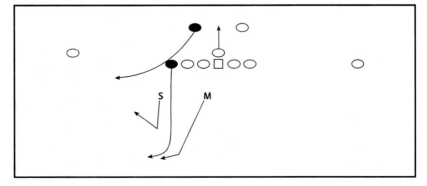

Figure 6-2b

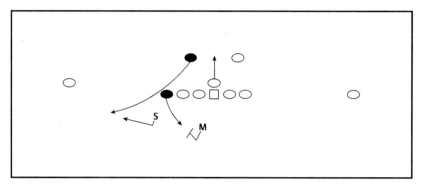

Figure 6-2c

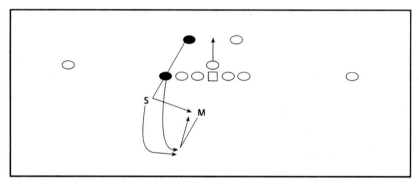

Figure 6-2d

Whom Can the Safety Help?

Although cover 1 employs a free safety, the two cornerbacks can't realistically count on the free safety to assist them with all deep patterns. The field is simply too wide to expect the free safety to cover the entire area between the sidelines. Cornerbacks who can expect inside help from the free safety should usually employ an outside-leverage technique. Cornerbacks, who can't expect inside help, should employ an inside-leverage technique. Figure 6-3 shows three common formation, strength/field position situations that determine the cornerback's leverage technique.

In Figure 6-3A, the strong cornerback cannot expect to receive inside help. Therefore, he maintains inside leverage on the flanker. The weak cornerback also employs an inside-leverage technique because the split end is so close to the sideline.

Because both receivers in Figure 6-3B have assumed tight splits, both cornerbacks can expect to receive inside help, so they maintain outside leverage.

Although the ball is in the middle of the field in Figure 6-3C, both the flanker and split end have assumed wide splits. The cornerbacks should therefore maintain inside leverage because it is doubtful that the safety can help either of them with inside routes.

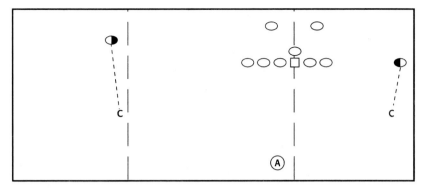

Figure 6-3a

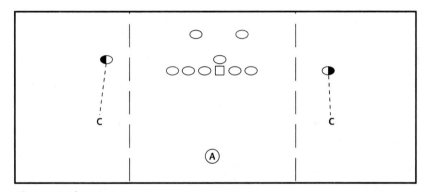

Figure 6-3b

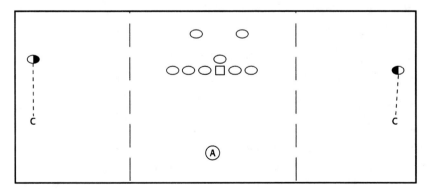

Figure 6-3c

STUNT #48

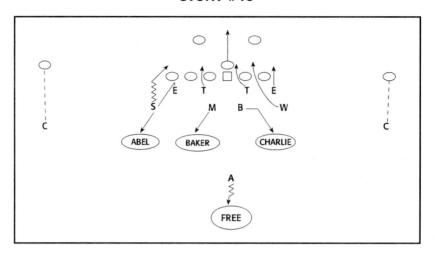

STUNT DESCRIPTION: This is a banjo blitz.

SECONDARY COVERAGE: Cover 1. The strong end, Mike, and Buck drop into coverage, and Assassin is free.

STUD: Creeps toward the line during cadence and rushes from the edge. Contains the quarterback and strongside run. Chases weakside run.

STRONG END: Plays 7 technique versus run. Drops **Abel** banjo versus pass.

STRONG TACKLE: Plays 3 technique.

MIKE: Plays base technique versus run. Drops **Baker** banjo versus pass.

BUCK: Scrapes outside and contains versus weakside run. Pursues strongside run from an inside-out position. Drops **Charlie** banjo versus pass.

WEAK TACKLE: Slants across the face of the offensive guard into the A gap.

WEAK END: Plays 7 technique versus run. Contains the quarterback versus pass.

WHIP: Blitzes through the B gap.

ASSASSIN: Provides alley support versus run. Free versus pass.

STRONG CORNER: Covers receiver #1 (inside/outside technique is dependent upon field position and the distance of #1's split).

WEAK CORNER: Covers receiver #1 (inside/outside technique is dependent upon field position and the distance of #1's split).

STUNT #49

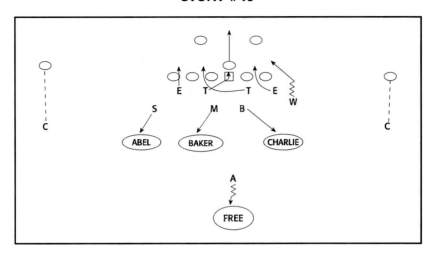

STUNT DESCRIPTION: This banjo blitz incorporates a tackle twist.

SECONDARY COVERAGE: Cover 1. Stud, Mike, and Buck drop into coverage, and Assassin is free.

STUD: Plays 8 technique versus run. Drops **Abel** banjo versus pass.

STRONG END: Plays 7 technique versus run. Contains the quarterback versus pass.

STRONG TACKLE: Slants to the near shoulder of the center and secures the strongside A gap.

MIKE: Plays base technique versus run. Drops **Baker** banjo versus pass.

BUCK: Pursues weakside and strongside run from an inside-out position. Drops **Charlie** banjo versus pass.

WEAK TACKLE: Loops across the face of the offensive guard and secures the strongside B gap.

WEAK END: Slants across the face of the offensive tackle into the B gap.

WHIP: Rushes from the edge. Contains the quarterback and weakside run. Chases strongside run.

ASSASSIN: Provides alley support versus run. Free versus pass.

STRONG CORNER: Covers receiver #1 (inside/outside technique is dependent upon field position and the distance of #1's split).

WEAK CORNER: Covers receiver #1 (inside/outside technique is dependent upon field position and the distance of #1's split).

STUNT #50

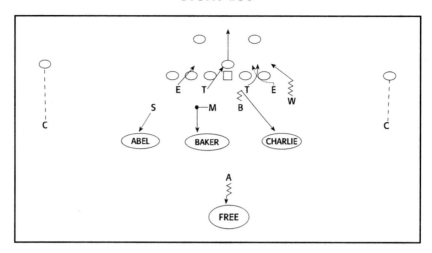

STUNT DESCRIPTION: This banjo blitz features a delayed weakside twin stunt.

SECONDARY COVERAGE: Cover 1. Stud, Mike, and Buck drop into coverage, and Assassin is free.

STUD: Plays 8 technique versus run. Drops **Abel** banjo versus pass.

STRONG END: Slants through the outside shoulder of the offensive tackle. Secures the C gap and contains the quarterback.

STRONG TACKLE: Slants across the face of the offensive guard into the A gap.

MIKE: Secures the B gap versus strongside run. Pursues weakside run from an inside-out position. Drops **Baker** banjo versus pass.

BUCK: Creeps toward the line during cadence and gives the impression that he's blitzing the A gap. Secures the A gap versus run and drops **Charlie** banjo versus pass.

WEAK TACKLE: Slants into the B gap.

WEAK END: Plays 7 technique versus run. Delay rushes through the B gap versus pass.

WHIP: Rushes from the edge. Contains the quarterback and strongside run. Chases weakside run.

ASSASSIN: Provides alley support versus run. Free versus pass.

STRONG CORNER: Covers receiver #1 (inside/outside technique is dependent upon field position and the distance of #1's split).

WEAK CORNER: Covers receiver #1 (inside/outside technique is dependent upon field position and the distance of #1's split).

STUNT #51

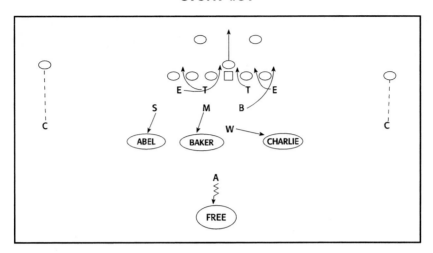

STUNT DESCRIPTION: This banjo blitz features a strongside line twist.

SECONDARY COVERAGE: Cover 1. Stud, Mike, and Buck drop into coverage, and Assassin is free.

STUD: Plays 8 technique versus run. Drops **Abel** banjo versus pass.

STRONG END: Loops across the face of the offensive guard into the strongside A gap. Strong end goes behind the slanting tackle.

STRONG TACKLE: Slants across the face of the offensive tackle into the strongside C gap. Secures the C gap versus run and contains the quarterback versus pass.

MIKE: Secures the B gap versus strongside run. Pursues weakside run from an inside-out position. Drops **Baker** banjo versus pass.

BUCK: Blitzes through the outside shoulder of the offensive tackle. Secures the C gap versus run and contains the quarterback versus pass.

WEAK TACKLE: Slants into the A gap.

WEAK END: Slants across the face of the offensive tackle into the B gap.

WHIP: Lines up in the "C" position. Scrapes outside and contains versus weakside run. Checks cutback versus strongside run. Drops **Charlie** banjo versus pass.

ASSASSIN: Provides alley support versus run. Free versus pass.

STRONG CORNER: Covers receiver #1 (inside/outside technique is dependent upon field position and the distance of #1's split).

WEAK CORNER: Covers receiver #1 (inside/outside technique is dependent upon field position and the distance of #1's split).

STUNT #52

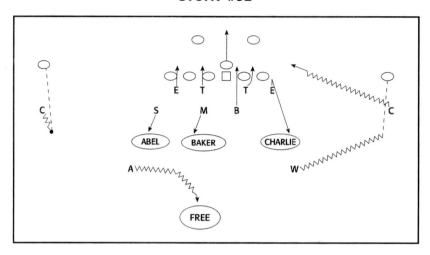

STUNT DESCRIPTION: This banjo blitz involves a weakside cornerback blitz.

SECONDARY COVERAGE: Cover 1 disguised as cover 2. Stud, Mike, and the weak end drop off into coverage.

STUD: Plays 8 technique versus run. Drops **Abel** banjo versus pass.

STRONG END: Plays 7 technique versus run. Contains the quarterback versus pass.

STRONG TACKLE: Plays 3 technique.

MIKE: Plays base technique versus run. Drops **Baker** banjo versus pass.

BUCK: Blitzes through the A gap.

WEAK TACKLE: Slants into the B gap.

WEAK END: Plays 7 technique versus run. Drops **Charlie** banjo versus pass.

WHIP: Lines up as though he's playing cover 2. During cadence, moves to a position that enables him to cover the split end (inside technique).

ASSASSIN: Lines up as though he's playing cover 2. Begins moving toward centerfield as Whip begins moving toward the split end. Provides alley support versus run. Free versus pass.

STRONG CORNER: Covers receiver #1 (inside /outside technique dependent upon field position and the receiver's split). Disguises his assignment as though he's playing cover 2.

WEAK CORNER: Disguises his assignment as cover 2. During cadence, slowly creeps inside and blitzes from the edge. Contains the quarterback and weakside run. Chases strongside run.

STUNT #53

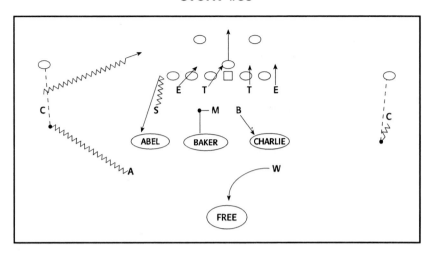

STUNT DESCRIPTION: This banjo blitz involves a strongside cornerback blitz.

SECONDARY COVERAGE: Cover 1 disguised as cover 2. Stud, Mike, and Buck drop off into coverage.

STUD: Creeps toward the line during cadence and gives the impression that he intends to rush from the edge. Plays 8 technique versus run. Drops **Abel** banjo versus pass.

STRONG END: Slants through the outside shoulder of the offensive tackle. Secures the C gap and contains the quarterback.

STRONG TACKLE: Slants into the A gap.

MIKE: Fills the B gap versus strongside run. Pursues weakside run from an inside-out position. Drops **Baker** banjo versus pass.

BUCK: Scrapes outside and contains weakside run. Pursues strongside run from an inside-out position. Drops **Charlie** banjo versus pass.

WEAK TACKLE: Plays 3 technique.

WEAK END: Plays 7 technique versus run. Contains the quarterback versus pass.

WHIP: Lines up as though he's playing cover 2. Begins moving toward centerfield as Assassin begins moving toward the flanker. Provides alley support versus run. Free versus pass.

ASSASSIN: Lines up as though he's playing cover 2. During cadence, moves to a position that enables him to cover the flanker (inside technique).

STRONG CORNER: Disguises his assignment as cover 2. During cadence, slowly creeps inside and blitzes from the edge. Contains the quarterback and strongside run. Chases weakside run.

WEAK CORNER: Covers receiver #1 (inside /outside technique dependent upon field position and the receiver's split). Disguises his assignment as though he's playing cover 2.

STUNT #54

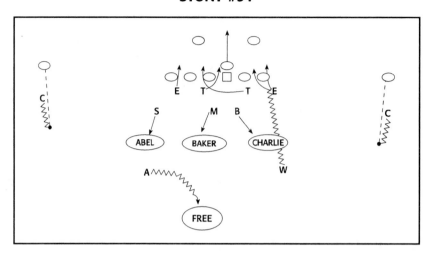

STUNT DESCRIPTION: This banjo blitz involves a weak safety (Whip) blitz.

SECONDARY COVERAGE: Cover 1 disguised as cover 2. Stud, Mike, and Buck drop off into coverage.

STUD: Plays 8 technique versus run. Drops **Abel** banjo versus pass. S

STRONG END: Plays 7 technique versus run. Contains the quarterback versus pass.

STRONG TACKLE: Slants into the A gap.

MIKE: Plays base technique versus run. Drops **Baker** banjo versus pass.

BUCK: Scrapes outside and contains weakside run. Pursues strongside run from an inside-out position. Drops **Charlie** banjo versus pass.

WEAK TACKLE: Loops across the face of the offensive guard into the strongside B gap.

WEAK END: Slants into the B gap.

WHIP: Lines up as though he's playing cover 2. Begins moving toward the line during cadence. At the snap, blitzes through the outside shoulder of the offensive tackle. Secures the C gap versus run and contains the quarterback versus pass.

ASSASSIN: Lines up as though he's playing cover 2. During cadence, moves toward centerfield. Free versus pass. Provides alley support versus run.

STRONG CORNER: Covers receiver #1 (inside /outside technique dependent upon field position and the receiver's split). Disguises his assignment as though he's playing cover 2.

WEAK CORNER: Covers receiver #1 (inside /outside technique dependent upon field position and the receiver's split). Disguises his assignment as though he's playing cover 2.

STUNT #55

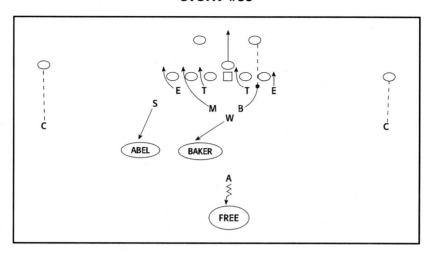

STUNT DESCRIPTION: This is a gumbo blitz.

SECONDARY COVERAGE: Cover 1. Stud and Whip drop into coverage, Buck spies the near back, and Assassin is free.

STUD: Plays 8 technique versus run. Drops **Abel** gumbo versus pass.

STRONG END: Slants across the face of the tight end. Contains the quarterback and strongside run. Chases weakside run.

STRONG TACKLE: Plays 3 technique.

MIKE: Blitzes through the outside shoulder of the offensive tackle and secures the C gap.

BUCK: Fakes a stunt toward the B gap. Secures the B gap versus run and spies the near back versus pass.

WEAK TACKLE: Slants into the A gap.

WEAK END: Plays 7 technique versus run. Contains the quarterback versus pass.

WHIP: Lines up in the "C" position. Scrapes outside and contains versus weakside run. Checks cutback versus strongside run. Drops **Charlie** banjo versus pass.

ASSASSIN: Provides alley support versus run. Free versus pass.

STRONG CORNER: Covers receiver #1 (inside/outside technique is dependent upon field position and the distance of #1's split).

WEAK CORNER: Covers receiver #1 (inside/outside technique is dependent upon field position and the distance of #1's split).

STUNT #56

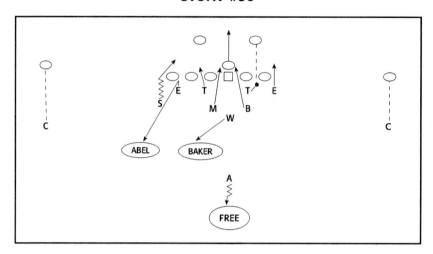

STUNT DESCRIPTION: This is a gumbo blitz.

SECONDARY COVERAGE: Cover 1. The strong end and Whip drop into coverage, the weak tackle spies the near back, and Assassin is free.

STUD: Creeps toward the line during cadence and rushes from the edge. Contains the quarterback and strongside run. Chases weakside run.

STRONG END: Plays 7 technique versus run. Drops **Abel** gumbo versus pass.

STRONG TACKLE: Slants into the B gap.

MIKE: Blitzes through the A gap.

BUCK: Blitzes through the A gap.

WEAK TACKLE: Slants into the B gap. Secures the B gap versus run and spies the near back versus pass.

WEAK END: Plays 7 technique versus run. Contains the quarterback versus pass.

WHIP: Lines up in the "C" position. Scrapes outside and contains versus weakside run. Checks for cutback versus strongside run. Drops **Baker** banjo versus pass.

ASSASSIN: Provides alley support versus run. Free versus pass.

STRONG CORNER: Covers receiver #1 (inside/outside technique is dependent upon field position and the distance of #1's split).

WEAK CORNER: Covers receiver #1 (inside/outside technique is dependent upon field position and the distance of #1's split).

STUNT #57

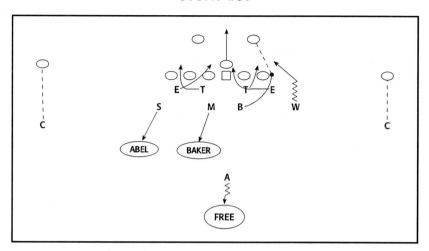

STUNT DESCRIPTION: This is a gumbo blitz.

SECONDARY COVERAGE: Cover 1. Stud and Mike drop into coverage, Buck spies the near back, and Assassin is free.

STUD: Plays 8 technique versus run. Drops **Abel** gumbo versus pass.

STRONG END: Slants through the outside shoulder of the offensive guard and controls the B gap.

STRONG TACKLE: Loops behind the end. Controls the C gap versus run and contains the quarterback versus pass.

MIKE: Plays base technique versus run. Drops **Baker** gumbo versus pass.

BUCK: Blitzes through the outside shoulder of the offensive tackle. Secures the C gap versus run and spies the near back versus pass.

WEAK TACKLE: Slants into the B gap.

WEAK END: Loops behind the tackle into the weakside A gap.

WHIP: Rushes from the edge. Contains the quarterback and weakside run. Chases strongside run.

ASSASSIN: Provides alley support versus run. Free versus pass.

STRONG CORNER: Covers receiver #1 (inside/outside technique is dependent upon field position and the distance of #1's split).

WEAK CORNER: Covers receiver #1 (inside /outside technique is dependent upon field position and the distance of #1's split).

STUNT #58

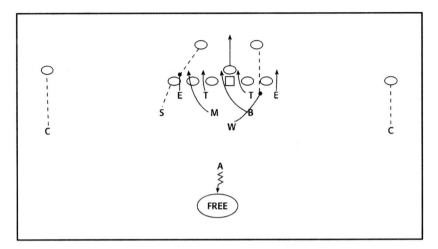

STUNT DESCRIPTION: This stunt gives the *illusion* of a seven-man pass rush. This is a good tactic versus strongside run and pass, but is vulnerable against weakside run.

SECONDARY COVERAGE: Cover 1. The strong end and Whip spy the two running backs, and Assassin is free.

STUD: Plays 8 technique versus run. Covers the tight end versus pass.

STRONG END: Plays 7 technique versus run. Spies the near back versus pass.

STRONG TACKLE: Slants into the B gap.

MIKE: Blitzes through the outside shoulder of the offensive tackle. Secures the C gap versus run and contains the quarterback versus pass.

BUCK: Blitzes through the strongside A gap.

WEAK TACKLE: Slants into the A gap.

WEAK END: Plays 7 technique versus run. Contains the quarterback versus pass.

WHIP: Lines up in the "C" position. Fakes a blitz toward the B gap. Secures the B gap versus run and spies the near back versus pass.

ASSASSIN: Provides alley support versus run. Free versus pass.

STRONG CORNER: Covers receiver #1 (inside/outside technique is dependent upon field position and the distance of #1's split).

WEAK CORNER: Covers receiver #1 (inside /outside technique is dependent upon field position and the distance of #1's split).

STUNT #59

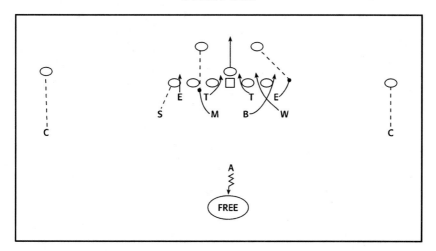

STUNT DESCRIPTION: This stunt gives the *illusion* of a seven-man pass rush.

SECONDARY COVERAGE: Cover 1. Mike and the weak end spy the two running backs, Stud covers the tight end, and Assassin is free.

STUD: Plays 8 technique versus run. Covers the tight end versus pass.

STRONG END: Plays 7 technique versus run. Contains the quarterback versus pass.

STRONG TACKLE: Slants into the A gap.

MIKE: Stunts toward the B gap. Secures the B gap versus run and spies the near back versus pass.

BUCK: Blitzes through the outside shoulder of the offensive tackle, contains the quarterback, and secures the C gap versus run.

WEAK TACKLE: Slants into the A gap.

WEAK END: Slants outside. Contains strongside run, chases weakside run, and spies the near back versus pass.

WHIP: Blitzes through the B gap.

ASSASSIN: Provides alley support versus run. Free versus pass.

STRONG CORNER: Covers receiver #1 (inside/outside technique is dependent upon field position and the distance of #1's split).

WEAK CORNER: Covers receiver #1 (inside /outside technique is dependent upon field position and the distance of #1's split).

STUNT #60

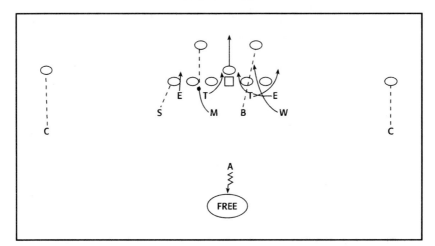

STUNT DESCRIPTION: This stunt gives the *illusion* of a seven-man pass rush and features a complex maze of defenders plugging gaps.

SECONDARY COVERAGE: Cover 1. Mike and Buck cover the two running backs, Stud covers the tight end, and Assassin is free.

STUD: Plays 8 technique versus run. Covers the tight end versus pass.

STRONG END: Plays 7 technique versus run. Contains the quarterback versus pass.

STRONG TACKLE: Slants into the A gap.

MIKE: Stunts toward the B gap. Secures the B gap versus run and spies the near back versus pass.

BUCK: Scrapes outside and contains versus weakside run. Pursues strongside run from an inside-out position, and covers the near back versus pass.

WEAK TACKLE: Slants across the face of the offensive tackle. Secures the C gap versus run and contains the quarterback versus pass.

WEAK END: Loops behind the offensive tackle into the weakside A gap.

WHIP: Blitzes through the B gap. Makes certain that his alignment is deep enough to allow the tackle to clear.

ASSASSIN: Provides alley support versus run. Free versus pass.

STRONG CORNER: Covers receiver #1 (inside/outside technique is dependent upon field position and the distance of #1's split).

WEAK CORNER: Covers receiver #1 (inside /outside technique is dependent upon field position and the distance of #1's split).

STUNT #61

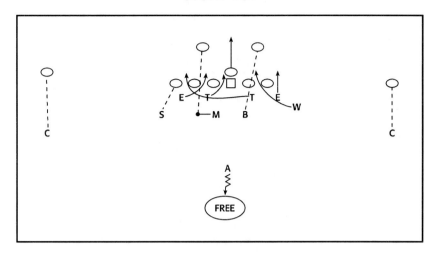

STUNT DESCRIPTION: This dog provides the defense with a five-man pass rush.

SECONDARY COVERAGE: Cover 1. Mike and Buck cover the two running backs, Stud covers the tight end, and Assassin is free.

STUD: Plays 8 technique versus run. Covers the tight end versus pass.

STRONG END: Slants across the face of the offensive tackle into the B gap.

STRONG TACKLE: Slants into the A gap.

MIKE: Shuffles slightly to the outside at the snap. Scrapes into the C gap versus strongside run. Pursues weakside run from an inside-out position. Covers the near back versus pass.

BUCK: Scrapes outside and contains versus weakside run. Pursues strongside run from an inside-out position. Covers the near back versus pass.

WEAK TACKLE: Slants across the face of the offensive tackle into the strongside C gap. Secures the C gap versus run and contains the quarterback versus pass.

WEAK END: Plays 7 technique versus run. Contains the quarterback versus pass.

WHIP: Blitzes through the B gap.

ASSASSIN: Provides alley support versus run. Free versus pass.

STRONG CORNER: Covers receiver #1 (inside/outside technique is dependent upon field position and the distance of #1's split).

WEAK CORNER: Covers receiver #1 (inside /outside technique is dependent upon field position and the distance of #1's split).

STUNT #62

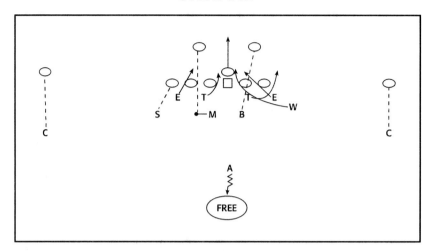

STUNT DESCRIPTION: This dog provides the defense with a five-man pass rush.

SECONDARY COVERAGE: Cover 1. Mike and Buck cover the two running backs, Stud covers the tight end, and Assassin is free.

STUD: Plays 8 technique versus run. Covers the tight end versus pass.

STRONG END: Slants through the outside shoulder of the offensive tackle. Secures the C gap and contains the quarterback.

STRONG TACKLE: Slants into the A gap.

MIKE: Secures the B gap versus run. Covers the near back versus pass.

BUCK: Scrapes outside and contains versus weakside run. Pursues strongside run from an inside-out position. Covers the near back versus pass.

WEAK TACKLE: Loops behind the end, secures the C gap, and contains the quarterback.

WEAK END: Slants across the face of the offensive tackle into the B gap.

WHIP: Blitzes through the A gap.

ASSASSIN: Provides alley support versus run. Free versus pass.

STRONG CORNER: Covers receiver #1 (inside/outside technique is dependent upon field position and the distance of #1's split).

WEAK CORNER: Covers receiver #1 (inside /outside technique is dependent upon field position and the distance of #1's split).

STUNT #63

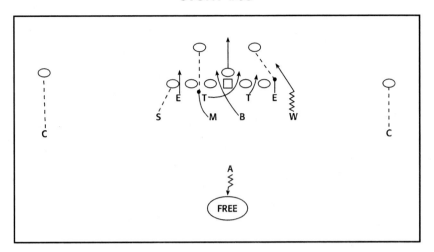

STUNT DESCRIPTION: This dog provides the defense with the illusion of a seven-man pass rush.

SECONDARY COVERAGE: Cover 1. Mike and the weak end cover the two running backs. Stud covers the tight end, and Assassin is free.

STUD: Plays 8 technique versus run. Covers the tight end versus pass.

STRONG END: Plays 7 technique versus run. Contains the quarterback versus pass.

STRONG TACKLE: Slants into the weakside A gap.

MIKE: Fakes a blitz toward the B gap and secures the B gap versus run. Covers the near back versus pass.

BUCK: Blitzes through the strongside A gap.

WEAK TACKLE: Slants into the B gap.

WEAK END: Plays 7 technique versus run. Spies the near back versus pass.

WHIP: Creeps toward the line during cadence and rushes from the edge. Contains the quarterback and weakside run. Chases strongside run.

ASSASSIN: Provides alley support versus run. Free versus pass.

STRONG CORNER: Covers receiver #1 (inside/outside technique is dependent upon field position and the distance of #1's split).

WEAK CORNER: Covers receiver #1 (inside /outside technique is dependent upon field position and the distance of #1's split).

STUNT #64

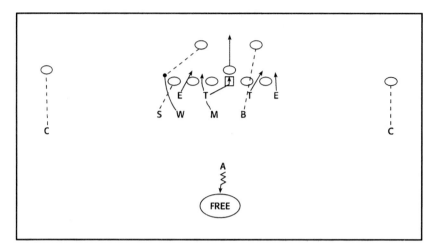

STUNT DESCRIPTION: This dog provides the defense with a good pass rush and strongside run support, but is vulnerable to weakside run.

SECONDARY COVERAGE: Cover 1. Whip and Buck cover the two running backs. Stud covers the tight end, and Assassin is free.

STUD: Plays 8 technique versus run. Covers the tight end versus pass.

STRONG END: Slants through the outside shoulder of the offensive tackle, secures the C gap, and contains the quarterback.

STRONG TACKLE: Slants to the near shoulder of the center and controls the strongside A gap.

MIKE: Blitzes through the B gap.

BUCK: Scrapes outside and contains versus weakside run. Pursues strongside run from an inside-out position. Covers the near back versus pass.

WEAK TACKLE: Slants into the B gap.

WEAK END: Plays 7 technique versus run. Contains the quarterback versus pass.

WHIP: Lines up in the "T" position. Fakes a blitz through the outside shoulder of the tight end. Contains strongside run and chases weakside run. Spies the near back versus pass.

ASSASSIN: Provides alley support versus run. Free versus pass.

STRONG CORNER: Covers receiver #1 (inside/outside technique is dependent upon field position and the distance of #1's split).

WEAK CORNER: Covers receiver #1 (inside /outside technique is dependent upon field position and the distance of #1's split).

STUNT #65

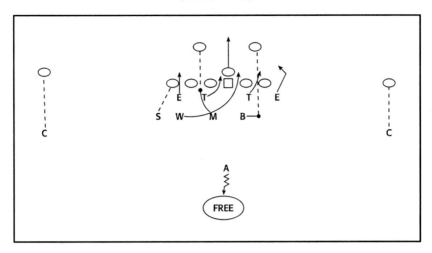

STUNT DESCRIPTION: This dog provides the defense with a five-man pass rush and is an excellent disguise of defensive intention.

SECONDARY COVERAGE: Cover 1. Mike and Buck cover the two running backs. Stud covers the tight end, and Assassin is free.

STUD: Plays 8 technique versus run. Covers the tight end versus pass.

STRONG END: Plays 7 technique versus run. Contains the quarterback versus pass.

STRONG TACKLE: Slants into the A gap.

MIKE: Fakes a blitz into the B gap. Secures the B gap versus run and spies the near back versus pass.

BUCK: Shuffles slightly to the outside at the snap. Scrapes into the C gap versus weakside run. Pursues strongside run from an inside-out position. Covers the near back versus pass.

WEAK TACKLE: Slants into the B gap.

WEAK END: Slants outside. Contains the quarterback and weakside run. Chases strongside run.

WHIP: Lines up in the "T" position and blitzes through the weakside A gap at the snap.

ASSASSIN: Provides alley support versus run. Free versus pass.

STRONG CORNER: Covers receiver #1 (inside/outside technique is dependent upon field position and the distance of #1's split).

WEAK CORNER: Covers receiver #1 (inside /outside technique is dependent upon field position and the distance of #1's split).

STUNT #66

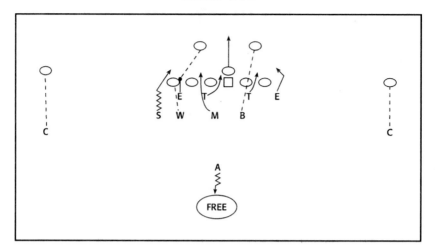

STUNT DESCRIPTION: This dog provides the defense with a five-man pass rush and excellent strongside run support, but is somewhat vulnerable versus weakside run.

SECONDARY COVERAGE: Cover 1. The strong end and Buck cover the two running backs. Whip covers the tight end, and Assassin is free.

STUD: Creeps toward the line during cadence and rushes from the edge. Contains the quarterback and strongside run. Chases weakside run.

STRONG END: Plays 7 technique versus run. Spies the near back versus pass.

STRONG TACKLE: Slants into the A gap.

MIKE: Blitzes through the B gap.

BUCK: Shuffles slightly to the outside at the snap. Scrapes into the C gap versus weakside run. Pursues strongside run from an inside-out position. Covers the near back versus pass.

WEAK TACKLE: Slants into the B gap.

WEAK END: Slants outside. Contains the quarterback and weakside run. Chases strongside run and contains the quarterback.

WHIP: Lines up in the "T" position and covers the tight end.

ASSASSIN: Provides alley support versus run. Free versus pass.

STRONG CORNER: Covers receiver #1 (inside/outside technique is dependent upon field position and the distance of #1's split).

WEAK CORNER: Covers receiver #1 (inside /outside technique is dependent upon field position and the distance of #1's split).

STUNT #67

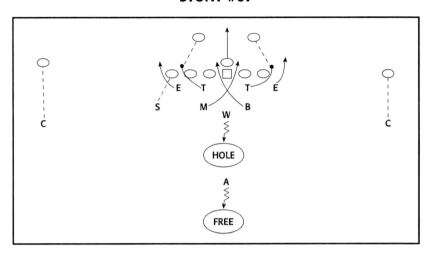

STUNT DESCRIPTION: This dog provides the defense with a five-man pass rush and excellent strongside and weakside run support.

SECONDARY COVERAGE: Cover 1 Robber. The tackles spy the two running backs. Stud covers the tight end, and Assassin is free.

STUD: Plays 8 technique versus run. Covers the tight end versus pass.

STRONG END: Slants across the face of the tight end. Contains the quarterback and strongside run. Chases weakside run.

STRONG TACKLE: Slants across the face of the offensive tackle. Secures the C gap versus run and spies the near back versus pass.

MIKE: Blitzes through the weakside A gap (Buck goes first).

BUCK: Blitzes through the strongside A gap.

WEAK TACKLE: Slants across the face of the offensive tackle. Secures the C gap versus run and spies the near back versus pass.

WEAK END: Slants outside. Contains the quarterback and weakside run. Chases strongside run.

WHIP: Lines up in the "C" position. Fills the flow-side B gap versus run. Robs the hole versus pass.

ASSASSIN: Provides alley support versus run. Free versus pass.

STRONG CORNER: Covers receiver #1 (inside/outside technique is dependent upon field position and the distance of #1's split).

WEAK CORNER: Covers receiver #1 (inside /outside technique is dependent upon field position and the distance of #1's split).

STUNT #68

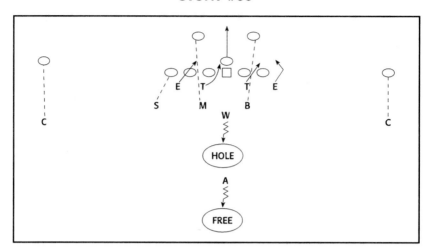

STUNT DESCRIPTION: This dog provides the defense with a weakside line slant and an extra defender to stop cutback.

SECONDARY COVERAGE: Cover 1 robber. Mike and Buck cover the two running backs. Stud covers the tight end, and Assassin is free.

STUD: Plays 8 technique versus run. Covers the tight end versus pass.

STRONG END: Slants through the outside shoulder of the offensive tackle. Secures the C gap versus run and contains the quarterback versus pass.

STRONG TACKLE: Slants into the A gap.

MIKE: Plays base technique versus run. Covers the near back versus pass.

BUCK: Scrapes into the C gap versus weakside run. Pursues strongside run from an inside-out position. Covers the near back versus pass.

WEAK TACKLE: Slants into the B gap.

WEAK END: Slants outside. Contains the quarterback and weakside run. Chases strongside run.

WHIP: Lines up in the "C" position. Shuffles down the line, checking cutback versus run. Robs the hole versus pass.

ASSASSIN: Provides alley support versus run. Free versus pass.

STRONG CORNER: Covers receiver #1 (inside/outside technique is dependent upon field position and the distance of #1's split).

WEAK CORNER: Covers receiver #1 (inside /outside technique is dependent upon field position and the distance of #1's split).

STUNT #69

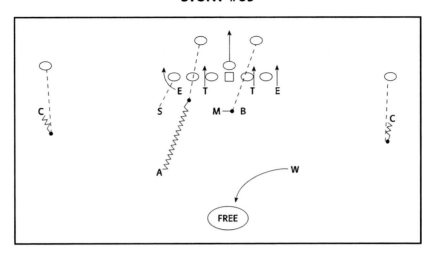

STUNT DESCRIPTION: This dog provides the defense with a fake safety blitz and good strongside run support, but it is vulnerable to weakside run.

SECONDARY COVERAGE: Cover 1 disguised as cover 2. Mike and Assassin cover the two running backs. Stud covers the tight end, and Whip is free.

STUD: Plays 8 technique versus run. Covers the tight end versus pass.

STRONG END: Slants across the face of the tight end. Contains the quarterback and strongside run. Chases weakside run.

STRONG TACKLE: Plays 3 technique.

MIKE: Shuffles to the head of the center. Pursues run from an inside-out position and covers the weakside halfback versus pass.

BUCK: Blitzes through the face of the center and controls both A gaps.

WEAK TACKLE: Plays 3 technique.

WEAK END: Plays 7 technique versus run. Contains the quarterback versus pass.

WHIP: Disguises his assignment as cover 2. Whip is free versus pass and has alley support versus run.

ASSASSIN: Lines up in a cover 2 disguise and slowly creeps toward the line during cadence. Gives the impression that he's blitzing strongside. Secures the C gap versus run and spies the near back versus pass.

STRONG CORNER: Covers receiver #1 disguised as cover 2 (inside/outside technique is dependent upon field position and the distance of #1's split).

WEAK CORNER: Covers receiver #1 disguised as cover 2 (inside /outside technique is dependent upon field position and the distance of #1's split).

STUNT #70

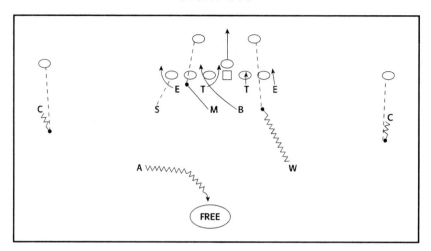

STUNT DESCRIPTION: This stunt provides the defense with a fake safety (Whip) blitz.

SECONDARY COVERAGE: Cover 1. Mike and Whip cover the two running backs. Stud covers the tight end, and Assassin is free.

STUD: Plays 8 technique versus run. Covers the tight end versus pass.

STRONG END: Slants across the face of the tight end. Contains the quarterback and strongside run. Chases weakside run.

STRONG TACKLE: Slants into the A gap.

MIKE: Fakes a blitz toward the C gap. Secures the C gap versus run and spies the near back versus pass.

BUCK: Blitzes through the outside shoulder of the guard and secures the strongside B gap.

WEAK TACKLE: Lines up in a 2 technique. Controls both the A and B gaps.

WEAK END: Plays 7 technique versus run. Contains the quarterback versus pass.

WHIP: Lines up in a cover 2 disguise and slowly creeps toward the line during cadence. Gives the impression that he's on a weakside blitz. Contains weakside run. Pursues strongside run from an inside-out position. Covers the near back versus pass.

ASSASSIN: Disguises his assignment as cover 2. Free versus pass and has alley support versus run.

STRONG CORNER: Covers receiver #1 disguised as cover 2 (inside/outside technique is dependent upon field position and the distance of #1's split).

WEAK CORNER: Covers receiver #1 disguised as cover 2 (inside /outside technique is dependent upon field position and the distance of #1's split).

STUNT #71

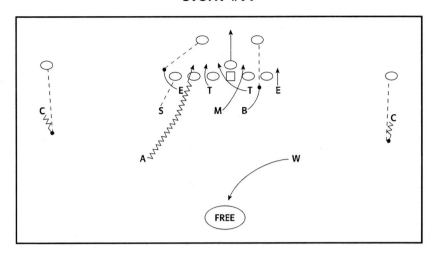

STUNT DESCRIPTION: This safety blitz provides the defense with the *illusion* of a seven-man pass rush.

SECONDARY COVERAGE: Cover 1. Buck and the strong end cover the two running backs. Stud covers the tight end, and Whip is free.

STUD: Covers the tight end.

STRONG END: Slants across the face of the tight end. Contains strongside run and chases weakside run. Spies the near back versus pass.

STRONG TACKLE: Plays 3 technique.

MIKE: Blitzes through the weakside A gap.

BUCK: Fakes a blitz into the weakside B gap. Secures the B gap versus run and spies the near back versus pass.

WEAK TACKLE: Slants across the center's face into the strongside A gap.

WEAK END: Plays 7 technique versus run. Contains the quarterback versus pass.

WHIP: Disguises his assignment as cover 2. Contains weakside run. Provides alley support for strongside run. Plays centerfield versus pass.

ASSASSIN: Lines up in a cover 2 disguise. Slowly creeps toward the line during cadence and blitzes through the outside shoulder of the offensive tackle. Secures the strongside C gap versus run and contains the quarterback versus pass.

STRONG CORNER: Covers receiver #1 disguised as cover 2 (inside/outside technique is dependent upon field position and the distance of #1's split).

WEAK CORNER: Covers receiver #1 disguised as cover 2 (inside /outside technique is dependent upon field position and the distance of #1's split).

STUNT #72

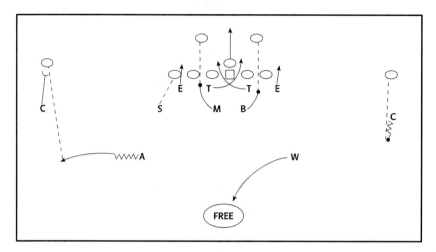

STUNT DESCRIPTION: This stunt provides the *illusion* of a six-man rush and provides double coverage on the flanker.

SECONDARY COVERAGE: Cover 1. Mike and Buck spy the two running backs. Stud covers the tight end, and Whip is free.

STUD: Plays 8 technique versus run. Covers the tight end versus pass.

STRONG END: Plays 7 technique versus run. Contains the quarterback versus pass.

STRONG TACKLE: Loops behind the weak tackle into the weakside A gap.

MIKE: Fakes a blitz into the B gap. Secures the B gap versus run, and spies the near back versus pass.

BUCK: Fakes a blitz into the B gap. Secures the B gap versus run, and spies the near back versus pass.

WEAK TACKLE: Slants across the center's face into the strongside A gap.

WEAK END: Plays 7 technique versus run. Contains the quarterback versus pass.

WHIP: Disguises his assignment as cover 2. Contains weakside run and provides alley support for strongside run. Plays centerfield versus pass.

ASSASSIN: Lines up in a cover 2 disguise and slowly creeps to a position that will enable him to cover the flanker's deep routes as the ball is snapped.

STRONG CORNER: Covers receiver #1. Jams him and funnels him inside.

WEAK CORNER: Covers receiver #1 disguised as cover 2 (inside /outside technique is dependent upon field position and the distance of #1's split).

CHAPTER 7

ZONE COVERAGE STUNTS

Before presenting the zone coverage stunts, this chapter begins with some explanations of the assignments, techniques, and pattern reads that defenders will utilize when employing the following zone drops:

* Curl-Out Drop

* Hook-Curl Drop

* Deep Middle Third Drop

* Deep Outside Third Drop

* Deep Half Drop

* Cornerback Cover 2 Zone Technique

CURL-OUT DROP

Versus a Pro Formation:

Defender should:

- Open up and aim for a spot ten yards deep, and in front of where receiver #1 originally lined up.

- Keep his head on a swivel and be aware of how many steps the QB takes.

- Adjust his drop to receiver #1's route.

- Listen for an "out-out" call by the defender dropping hook-curl, and an "in-in" call by the corners.

- Play the deepest receiver in his zone and rally up to the short routes after the ball has been thrown.

Versus Quick 3-Step Patterns (Hitches, Outs, Slants, etc.):

Defender should:

- Try to get into the throwing lane.

- Arrive in time to punish the receiver and strip the ball, even if he arrives too late to intercept or tip the pass. Remember that wide receivers are usually not the most courageous players on the field. Discourage them from entering that zone again.

Versus 5- and 7-Step Out and Comeback Routes:

Defender should:

- Play under these routes from an inside-out position

- Get into the throwing lane and force the quarterback to throw the ball high.

- Strip the ball and punish the receiver.

Versus the Curl:

Defender should:

- Remember that this pattern is usually accompanied by an out by receiver #2.

- Set up in a position three yards inside of, and underneath, the curl, trying to maintain an inside-out-and-under position on both the receiver and the ball.

- Gradually widen out, but not jump the out pattern too quickly if receiver #2's route crosses his face. He must make sure that he has received help from the defender who is dropping hook-curl first. If the defender jumps the out too quickly, he will be giving up a 12- to 18-yard pattern in order to stop a 5-yard pattern.

Versus the Post, Post-Corner, and Streak Routes:

Defender should:

- Check receiver #2 and listen for an "out-out" call if receiver #1 runs a vertical route (streak, fade, post-corner, etc.).

- Run with the vertical route and, if possible, collision it, if no "out-out" call occurs. The defensive player should look over his inside shoulder to find the ball.

- Try to get under the route, when getting a "post" call from the corner, if receiver #2 does not threaten him.

HOOK-CURL DROP

Defender should:

- Open outside and drop 12- to 15-yards deep.

- Let the field position and the formation determine the width of his drop.

- Read #2-#1 versus a pro formation, and listen for a "cross" call from the other defender who is dropping hook-curl.

- Play the deepest receiver in his zone, when dropping hook-curl, and rally up to the short receivers.

Versus a Vertical Release by Receiver #2:

Defender should:

- Get to a point one yard inside and underneath the receiver.

- Wall off a receiver who hooks inside by using a hand shove. The defender cannot let the receiver get into the middle hook zone.

- Break for an inside-out position and try to strip the ball if the receiver hooks outside.

- Collision a receiver who streaks, and stay with him until 18 yards from the line of scrimmage, and then sink. If the defender gets an "in-in" call from the other defender who is dropping hook-curl, he should hang in the hook and play the deepest receiver. If no "in-in" call is made, he checks curl.

Versus Flare or Flat Release by Receiver #2:

Defender should:

- Sprint to the curl and locate the widest receiver.

- Give an "out-out" call.

- Get to a point three yards inside and underneath the widest receiver, if he's running a curl.

- Maintain an inside-out position.

- Pivot inside and get additional depth, if the widest receiver runs a post.

Versus a Crossing Route by Receiver #2:

Defender should:

- Try to ward off the receiver if he crosses deeper than five yards, by jamming him as far as the center. As the defender releases him, he calls "cross".

- Square up and continue to drop if the receiver crosses shallow. Call "cross" and look for a complementary crossing route by the #2 receiver from the opposite side, or a curl or post by receiver #1.

Versus a Seam by Receiver #2:

Defender should:

- Expect to see this route more often when playing sprint–out teams.

- Get additional width and make his drop to the receiver.

- Get into the throwing lane.

- Sprint for the receiver's outside hip and come underneath.

Versus Play Action:

Defender should:

- Open outside and read the widest receiver, when aligned on the playside.

- Recognize that the ball is in the pocket and the possibility of a throwback exists, when aligned on the backside.

- Open and get under the curl or post.

- React up to crossing patterns from the opposite side.

Versus Sprint, Waggle or Bootleg:

Defender should:

- Open outside and read receiver #2, when aligned on the playside.

- Recognize that the ball is out of the pocket and the possibility of a throwback exists, when aligned on the backside.

- Drop to deep middle hook and slide with the quarterback. Locate and cover crossing patterns.

DEEP MIDDLE THIRD DROP

Defender should:

- Key the ball to the receivers.

- Shuffle two steps in the direction of the ball.

- Adjust his drop angle to put himself midway between the corners versus a dropback pass.

- Key the tight end's release versus the pro formation.

  - If the tight end goes vertical, the defender must be prepared to go deep.

  - If the tight end releases short or away from the defender, he looks for post from the two widest receivers. Remember, a defender can't react to a short or intermediate route as long as there is a deep threat.

DEEP OUTSIDE THIRD DROP

Defender should:

- Key the ball to the receiver.

- See #1 and #2 receivers to his side versus a dropback pass.

- Control the speed of his backpedal, if both receivers run short or intermediate routes, so he is in a good position to break on the ball.

- Read receiver #2, if #1 runs a short or intermediate route, since #2 can threaten him deep.

- Squeeze the field, keeping outside leverage on the deepest receiver, if both #1 and #2 receivers go away.

DEEP HALF DROP

Defender should:

- Stay as deep as the deepest receiver.

- Read both #1 and #2, and work toward the receiver who goes deep.

- Move outside of #2, if both receivers go deep, so that he will be able to break to #1.

CORNERBACK'S COVER 2 ZONE TECHNIQUE

Defender should:

- Jam receiver #1. Stay on his outside shoulder and funnel him inside. Not allow #1 an outside release.

- See the release of receiver #2.

  - If #2 releases short and into the flat, gain depth and width. The defender should not react to #2 until he crosses the defender's face.

  - If #2 runs the wheel route, collision and run with him.

  - If #2 runs a vertical or crossing route, stay with #1 unless threatened by #3. If #3 releases into the flats, the defender must be in a position to rally up.

STUNT #73

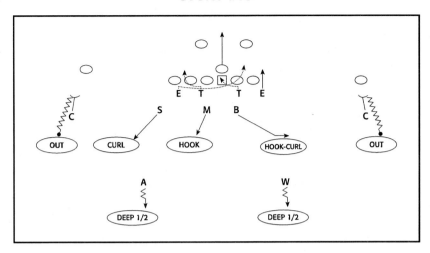

STUNT DESCRIPTION: This delayed line twist is a reaction to pass.

SECONDARY COVERAGE: Five-under, two-deep zone.

STUD: Plays 8 technique versus run. Drops *curl* versus pass.

STRONG END: Plays 7 technique versus run. Loops through the outside shoulder of the weakside guard versus pass.

STRONG TACKLE: Plays 3 technique versus run. Attacks the outside shoulder of the offensive tackle and contains the quarterback versus pass.

MIKE: Plays base technique versus run. Drops *hook* versus pass.

BUCK: Plays base technique versus run. Drops *hook-curl* versus pass.

WEAK TACKLE: Plays 3 technique versus run. Attacks the near shoulder of the center versus pass.

WEAK END: Plays 7 technique versus run. Contains the quarterback versus pass.

WHIP: Plays deep-half coverage.

ASSASSIN: Plays deep-half coverage.

STRONG CORNER: Jams receiver #1 inside and sinks to the *out*.

WEAK CORNER: Jams receiver #1 inside and sinks to the *out*.

STUNT #74

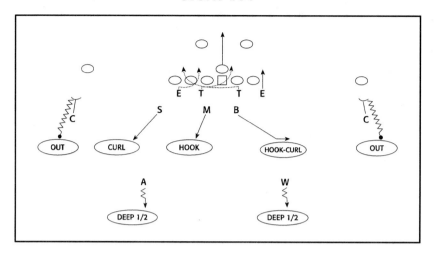

STUNT DESCRIPTION: This delayed line twist is a reaction to pass.

SECONDARY COVERAGE: Five-under, two-deep zone.

STUD: Plays 8 technique versus run. Drops *curl* versus pass.

STRONG END: Plays 7 technique versus run. Attacks the inside shoulder of the offensive tackle versus pass.

STRONG TACKLE: Plays 3 technique versus run. Attacks the far shoulder of the center versus pass.

MIKE: Plays base technique versus run. Drops *hook* versus pass.

BUCK: Plays base technique versus run. Drops *hook-curl* versus pass.

WEAK TACKLE: Plays 3 technique versus run. Attacks the far shoulder of the strongside offensive tackle and contains the quarterback versus pass.

WEAK END: Plays 7 technique versus run. Contains the quarterback versus pass.

WHIP: Plays deep-half coverage.

ASSASSIN: Plays deep-half coverage.

STRONG CORNER: Jams receiver #1 inside and sinks to the *out*.

WEAK CORNER: Jams receiver #1 inside and sinks to the *out*.

STUNT #75

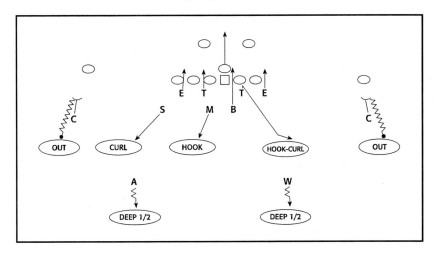

STUNT DESCRIPTION: This is an "old school" zone blitz in which the weak tackle drops into coverage versus pass.

SECONDARY COVERAGE: Five-under, two-deep zone.

STUD: Plays 8 technique versus run. Drops *curl* versus pass.

STRONG END: Plays 7 technique versus run. Contains the quarterback versus pass.

STRONG TACKLE: Plays 3 technique.

MIKE: Plays base technique versus run. Drops *hook* versus pass.

BUCK: Blitzes through the A gap.

WEAK TACKLE: Plays 3 technique versus run. Drops *hook-curl* versus pass.

WEAK END: Plays 7 technique versus run. Contains the quarterback versus pass.

WHIP: Plays deep-half coverage.

ASSASSIN: Plays deep-half coverage.

STRONG CORNER: Jams receiver #1 inside and sinks to the *out*.

WEAK CORNER: Jams receiver #1 inside and sinks to the *out*.

STUNT #76

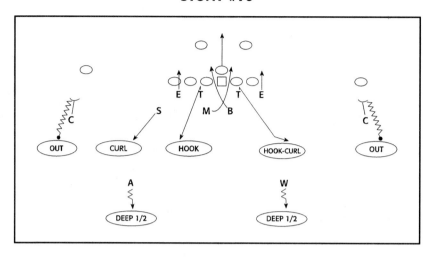

STUNT DESCRIPTION: This is an "old school" zone blitz in which both tackles drop into coverage versus pass.

SECONDARY COVERAGE: Five-under, two-deep zone.

STUD: Plays 8 technique versus run. Drops *curl* versus pass.

STRONG END: Plays 7 technique versus run. Contains the quarterback versus pass.

STRONG TACKLE: Plays 3 technique versus run. Drops *hook* versus pass.

MIKE: Blitzes through the weakside A gap. Buck goes first.

BUCK: Blitzes through the strongside A gap.

WEAK TACKLE: Plays 3 technique versus run. Drops *hook-curl* versus pass.

WEAK END: Plays 7 technique versus run. Contains the quarterback versus pass.

WHIP: Plays deep-half coverage.

ASSASSIN: Plays deep-half coverage.

STRONG CORNER: Jams receiver #1 inside and sinks to the *out*.

WEAK CORNER: Jams receiver #1 inside and sinks to the *out*.

STUNT #77

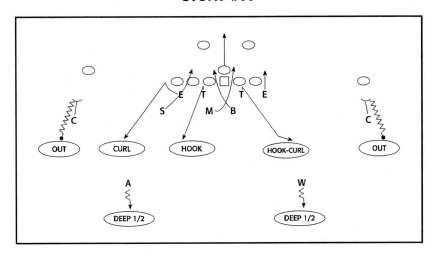

STUNT DESCRIPTION: This is an "old school" zone blitz in which both tackles and the strong end drop into coverage versus pass.

SECONDARY COVERAGE: Five-under, two-deep zone.

STUD: Blitzes through the outside shoulder of the offensive tackle, secures the C gap, and contains the quarterback.

STRONG END: Slants across the face of the tight end. Contains strongside run and chases weakside run. Drops *curl* versus pass.

STRONG TACKLE: Plays 3 technique versus run. Drops *hook* versus pass.

MIKE: Blitzes through the weakside A gap. Buck goes first.

BUCK: Blitzes through the strongside A gap.

WEAK TACKLE: Plays 3 technique versus run. Drops *hook-curl* versus pass.

WEAK END: Plays 7 technique versus run. Contains the quarterback versus pass.

WHIP: Plays deep-half coverage.

ASSASSIN: Plays deep-half coverage.

STRONG CORNER: Jams receiver #1 inside and sinks to the *out*.

WEAK CORNER: Jams receiver #1 inside and sinks to the *out*.

STUNT #78

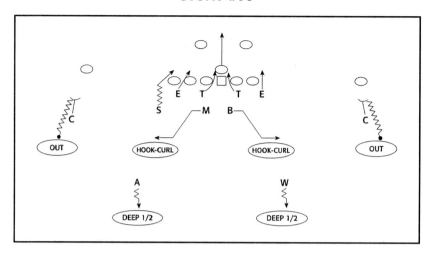

STUNT DESCRIPTION: This dog has Stud rushing from the edge.

SECONDARY COVERAGE: Four-under, two-deep zone.

STUD: Creeps toward the line during cadence and rushes from the edge. Contains the quarterback and strongside run. Chases weakside run.

STRONG END: Slants through the near shoulder of the offensive tackle and secures the C gap.

STRONG TACKLE: Slants across the face of the offensive guard into the A gap.

MIKE: Plugs the B gap versus strongside run. Pursues weakside run from an inside-out position. Drops *hook-curl* versus pass.

BUCK: Plugs the B gap versus strongside run. Pursues weakside run from an inside-out position. Drops *hook-curl* versus pass.

WEAK TACKLE: Slants across the face of the offensive guard into the A gap.

WEAK END: Plays 7 technique versus run. Contains the quarterback versus pass.

WHIP: Plays deep-half coverage.

ASSASSIN: Plays deep-half coverage.

STRONG CORNER: Jams receiver #1 inside and sinks to the *out*.

WEAK CORNER: Jams receiver #1 inside and sinks to the *out*.

STUNT #79

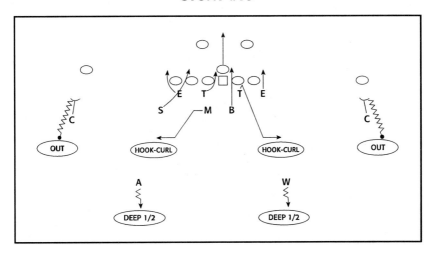

STUNT DESCRIPTION: This is an "old school" zone blitz in which the weak tackle drops into coverage versus pass.

SECONDARY COVERAGE: Four-under, two-deep zone.

STUD: Blitzes through the outside shoulder of the offensive tackle, secures the C gap, and contains the quarterback.

STRONG END: Slants across the face of the tight end. Contains the quarterback and strongside run. Chases weakside run.

STRONG TACKLE: Slants across the face of the offensive guard into the A gap.

MIKE: Plugs the B gap versus strongside run. Pursues weakside run from an inside-out position. Drops *hook-curl* versus pass.

BUCK: Blitzes through the A gap.

WEAK TACKLE: Plays 3 technique versus run. Drops *hook-curl* versus pass.

WEAK END: Plays 7 technique versus run. Contains the quarterback versus pass.

WHIP: Plays deep-half coverage.

ASSASSIN: Plays deep-half coverage.

STRONG CORNER: Jams receiver #1 inside and sinks to the *out*.

WEAK CORNER: Jams receiver #1 inside and sinks to the *out*.

STUNT #80

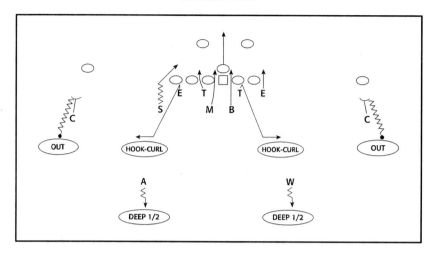

STUNT DESCRIPTION: This is an "old school" zone blitz in which the strong end and weak tackle drop into coverage versus pass.

SECONDARY COVERAGE: Four-under, two-deep zone.

STUD: Creeps toward the line during cadence and rushes from the edge. Contains the quarterback and strongside run. Chases weakside run.

STRONG END: Plays 7 technique versus run. Drops *hook-curl* versus pass.

STRONG TACKLE: Slants into the B gap.

MIKE: Blitzes through the A gap.

BUCK: Blitzes through the A gap.

WEAK TACKLE: Plays 3 technique versus run. Drops *hook-curl* versus pass.

WEAK END: Plays 7 technique versus run. Contains the quarterback versus pass.

WHIP: Plays deep-half coverage.

ASSASSIN: Plays deep-half coverage.

STRONG CORNER: Jams receiver #1 inside and sinks to the *out*.

WEAK CORNER: Jams receiver #1 inside and sinks to the *out*.

STUNT #81

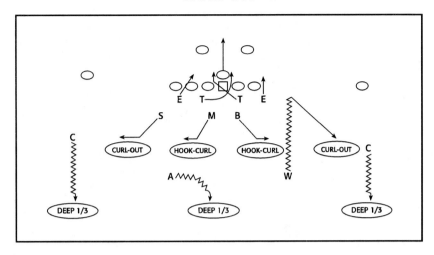

STUNT DESCRIPTION: This stunt features a fake safety blitz and a line twist that is executed at the snap of the ball.

SECONDARY COVERAGE: Cover 3 sky disguised as cover 2.

STUD: Plays 8 technique versus run. Drops *curl-out* versus pass.

STRONG END: Slants through the near shoulder of the offensive tackle. Controls the C gap and contains the quarterback.

STRONG TACKLE: Loops behind the weak tackle into the weakside A gap.

MIKE: Plays base technique versus run. Drops *hook-curl* versus pass.

BUCK: Plays base technique versus run. Drops *hook-curl* versus pass.

WEAK TACKLE: Slants inside and attacks the far shoulder of the center. Secures the strongside A gap.

WEAK END: Plays 7 technique versus run. Contains the quarterback versus pass.

WHIP: Lines up as though he's playing cover2. During cadence, creeps toward the line as though he's going to blitz. Contains weakside run. Checks for cutback versus strongside run and drops *curl-out* versus pass.

ASSASSIN: Lines up as though he's playing cover 2. Provides alley support for strongside run and drops deep middle-third coverage versus pass.

STRONG CORNER: Plays deep outside-third coverage.

WEAK CORNER: Plays deep outside-third coverage.

STUNT #82

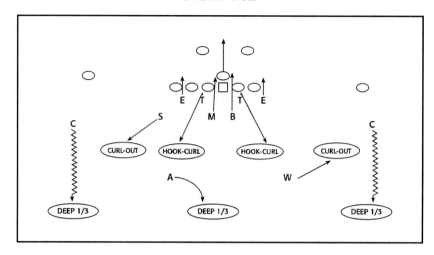

STUNT DESCRIPTION: This is an "old school" zone blitz in which both tackles drop off into coverage.

SECONDARY COVERAGE: Cover 3 sky disguised as cover 2.

STUD: Plays 8 technique versus run. Drops *curl-out* versus pass.

STRONG END: Plays 7 technique versus run. Contains the quarterback versus pass.

STRONG TACKLE: Plays 3 technique versus run. Drops *hook-curl* versus pass.

MIKE: Blitzes through the A gap.

BUCK: Blitzes through the A gap.

WEAK TACKLE: Plays 3 technique versus run. Drops *hook-curl* versus pass.

WEAK END: Plays 7 technique versus run. Contains the quarterback versus pass.

WHIP: Lines up as though he's playing cover 2. Contains weakside run. Checks for cutback versus strongside run and drops *curl-out* versus pass.

ASSASSIN: Lines up as though he's playing cover 2. Provides alley support for strongside run and drops deep middle-third coverage versus pass.

STRONG CORNER: Plays deep outside-third coverage.

WEAK CORNER: Plays deep outside-third coverage.

STUNT #83

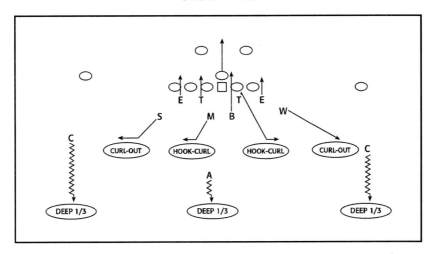

STUNT DESCRIPTION: This is an "old school" zone blitz in which the weak tackle drops off into coverage.

SECONDARY COVERAGE: Cover 3.

STUD: Plays 8 technique versus run. Drops *curl-out* versus pass.

STRONG END: Plays 7 technique versus run. Contains the quarterback versus pass.

STRONG TACKLE: Plays 3 technique.

MIKE: Plays base technique versus run. Drops *hook-curl* versus pass.

BUCK: Blitzes through the A gap.

WEAK TACKLE: Plays 3 technique versus run. Drops *hook-curl* versus pass.

WEAK END: Plays 7 technique versus run. Contains the quarterback versus pass.

WHIP: Plays 8 technique versus run. Drops *curl-out* versus pass.

ASSASSIN: Plays deep middle-third coverage.

STRONG CORNER: Plays deep outside-third coverage.

WEAK CORNER: Plays deep outside-third coverage.

CHAPTER 8

ADAPTING THE STUNT GAME TO EMPTY AND ACEBACK FORMATIONS

STUNT #84

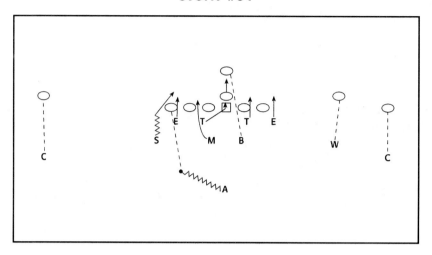

STUNT DESCRIPTION: This is a strongside *overload* versus an aceback formation.

SECONDARY COVERAGE: Zero coverage disguised as cover 1.

STUD: Creeps toward the line during cadence and rushes from the edge. Contains the quarterback and strongside run. Chases weakside run.

STRONG END: Plays 7 technique.

STRONG TACKLE: Slants into the near shoulder of the center and secures the strongside A gap. It is vital that the strong tackle crush the center's body into the weakside A gap versus weakside run, or the defense will be vulnerable to cutback.

MIKE: Blitzes through the B gap.

BUCK: Plays base technique versus run. Covers the aceback versus pass.

WEAK TACKLE: Plays 3 technique.

WEAK END: Plays 7 technique versus run. Contains the quarterback versus pass.

WHIP: Covers receiver #2 (inside technique–lower level).

ASSASSIN: Covers the tight end. Disguises his assignment as cover 1.

STRONG CORNER: Covers receiver #1 (inside technique).

WEAK CORNER: Covers receiver #1 (inside technique–upper level).

STUNT #85

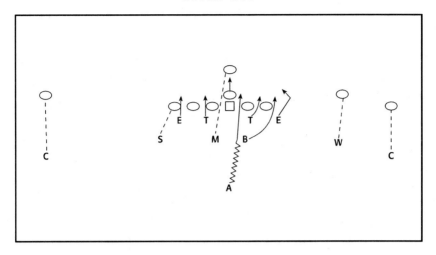

STUNT DESCRIPTION: This is a weakside *overload* with an Assassin blitz. This is a good stunt to use in a passing situation or when a team has a tendency to run toward the split end.

SECONDARY COVERAGE: A variation of zero coverage in which Stud covers the tight end.

STUD: Covers the tight end.

STRONG END: Plays 7 technique versus run. Contains the quarterback versus pass.

STRONG TACKLE: Plays 3 technique.

MIKE: Plays base technique versus run. Covers the near back versus pass.

BUCK: Blitzes through the outside shoulder of the tackle and secures the C gap.

WEAK TACKLE: Slants into the B gap.

WEAK END: Slants outside. Contains the quarterback and weakside run. Chases strongside run.

WHIP: Covers receiver #2 (inside technique–lower level).

ASSASSIN: Creeps toward the line during cadence and blitzes through the weakside A gap.

STRONG CORNER: Covers receiver #1 (inside technique).

WEAK CORNER: Covers receiver #1 (inside technique–upper level).

STUNT #86

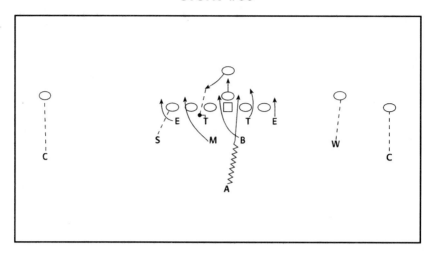

STUNT DESCRIPTION: This is a strongside *illusion* with an Assassin blitz. This is a good stunt to use in a passing situation or when a team has a tendency to run toward the tight end.

SECONDARY COVERAGE: A variation of zero coverage in which Stud covers the tight end.

STUD: Covers the tight end.

STRONG END: Slants across the face of the tight end. Contains the quarterback and strongside run. Chases weakside run.

STRONG TACKLE: Plays 3 technique versus run. Spies ace versus pass. If ace blocks weak, the strong tackle continues to rush.

MIKE: Blitzes through the outside shoulder of the offensive tackle and secures the C gap.

BUCK: Blitzes through the strongside A gap.

WEAK TACKLE: Plays 3 technique versus run. Spies ace versus pass. If ace blocks strong, the weak tackle continues to rush.

WEAK END: Plays 7 technique versus run. Contains the quarterback versus pass.

WHIP: Covers receiver #2 (inside technique–lower level).

ASSASSIN: Creeps toward the line during cadence and blitzes through the weakside A gap.

STRONG CORNER: Covers receiver #1 (inside technique).

WEAK CORNER: Covers receiver #1 (inside technique–upper level).

STUNT #87

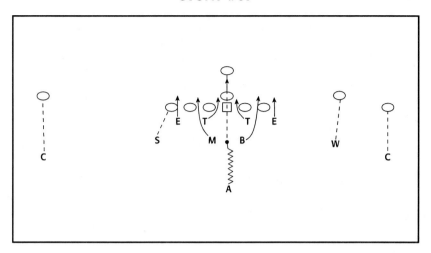

STUNT DESCRIPTION: This stunt gives the *illusion* of a six-man pass rush and threatens an assassin blitz.

SECONDARY COVERAGE: A variation of zero coverage in which Stud covers the tight end.

STUD: Covers the tight end.

STRONG END: Plays 7 technique versus run. Contains the quarterback versus pass.

STRONG TACKLE: Slants into the A gap.

MIKE: Blitzes through the B gap

BUCK: Blitzes through the B gap.

WEAK TACKLE: Slants into the A gap.

WEAK END: Plays 7 technique versus run. Contains the quarterback versus pass.

WHIP: Covers receiver #2 (inside technique–lower level).

ASSASSIN: Creeps toward the line during cadence and gives the impression that he's going to blitz. Spies the aceback versus pass, and provides alley support versus run.

STRONG CORNER: Covers receiver #1 (inside technique).

WEAK CORNER: Covers receiver #1 (inside technique–upper level).

STUNT #88

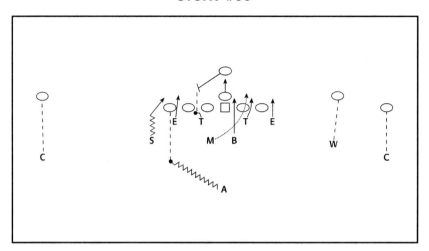

STUNT DESCRIPTION: This is a delay blitz that provides a weakside overload.

SECONDARY COVERAGE: Zero coverage disguised as cover 1.

STUD: Creeps toward the line during cadence and rushes from the edge. Contains the quarterback and strongside run. Chases weakside run.

STRONG END: Plays 7 technique.

STRONG TACKLE: Plays 3 technique versus run. Spies ace versus pass. If ace blocks weak, the strong tackle continues to rush.

MIKE: Plays base technique versus run. Delay blitzes through the weakside B gap versus pass.

BUCK: Blitzes through the A gap.

WEAK TACKLE: Plays 3 technique versus run. Spies ace versus pass. If ace blocks strong, the weak tackle continues to rush.

WEAK END: Plays 7 technique versus run. Contains the quarterback versus pass.

WHIP: Covers receiver #2 (inside technique–lower level).

ASSASSIN: Covers the tight end. Disguises his assignment by giving the quarterback a cover 1 pre-snap read.

STRONG CORNER: Covers receiver #1 (inside technique).

WEAK CORNER: Covers receiver #1 (inside technique–upper level).

STUNT #89

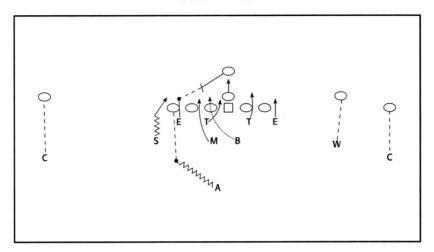

STUNT DESCRIPTION: This is a delay blitz that provides a strongside overload.

SECONDARY COVERAGE: Zero coverage.

STUD: Creeps toward the line during cadence and rushes from the edge. Contains the quarterback and strongside run. Chases weakside run.

STRONG END: Plays 7 technique versus run. Spies ace versus pass. If ace blocks weak, the strong end continues to rush.

STRONG TACKLE: Slants into the A gap.

MIKE: Blitzes through the B gap.

BUCK: Plays base technique versus run. Delay blitzes through the strongside B gap versus pass.

WEAK TACKLE: Plays 3 technique versus run. Spies ace versus pass. If ace blocks strong, the weak tackle continues to rush.

WEAK END: Plays 7 technique versus run. Contains the quarterback versus run.

WHIP: Covers receiver #2 (inside technique–lower level).

ASSASSIN: Covers the tight end. Disguises his assignment by giving the quarterback a cover 1 pre-snap read.

STRONG CORNER: Covers receiver #1 (inside technique).

WEAK CORNER: Covers receiver #1 (inside technique–upper level).

STUNT #90

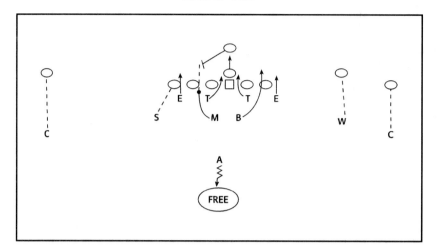

STUNT DESCRIPTION: This stunt gives the *illusion* of a six-man pass rush. Possible variation: Mike and Buck blitz the A gaps, and the tackles spy.

SECONDARY COVERAGE: Cover 1. Mike and Buck spy ace, and Stud covers the tight end.

STUD: Covers the tight end.

STRONG END: Plays 7 technique versus run. Contains the quarterback versus pass.

STRONG TACKLE: Slants into the A gap.

MIKE: Fakes a blitz toward the B gap. Secures the B gap versus run and spies the near back versus pass. If ace blocks weak, Mike continues to blitz.

BUCK: Fakes a blitz toward the B gap. Secures the B gap versus run and spies the near back versus pass. If ace blocks strong, Buck continues to blitz.

WEAK TACKLE: Slants into the A gap.

WEAK END: Plays 7 technique versus run. Contains the quarterback versus pass.

WHIP: Covers receiver #2 (inside technique–lower level).

ASSASSIN: Provides alley support versus run. Plays centerfield versus pass.

STRONG CORNER: Covers receiver #1 (inside technique).

WEAK CORNER: Covers receiver #1 (inside technique–upper level).

STUNT #91

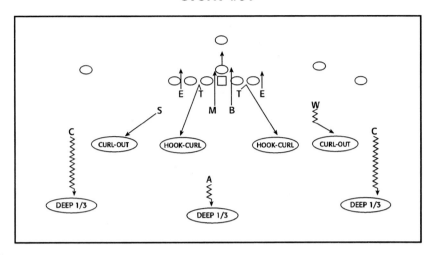

STUNT DESCRIPTION: This is an "old school" zone blitz in which the tackles drop off into coverage.

SECONDARY COVERAGE: Cover 3.

STUD: Plays 8 technique versus run. Drops *curl-out* versus pass.

STRONG END: Plays 7 technique versus run. Contains the quarterback versus pass.

STRONG TACKLE: Plays 3 technique versus run. Drops *hook-curl* versus pass.

MIKE: Blitzes through the A gap.

BUCK: Blitzes through the A gap.

WEAK TACKLE: Plays 3 technique versus run. Drops *hook-curl* versus pass.

WEAK END: Plays 7 technique versus run. Contains the quarterback versus pass.

WHIP: Reads the ball. His first priority is to deny receiver #2 a quick seam route. Supports weakside run after he has taken care of his number one priority. Drops *curl-out* versus dropback pass.

ASSASSIN: Plays deep middle-third coverage.

STRONG CORNER: Plays deep outside-third coverage.

WEAK CORNER: Plays deep outside-third coverage.

STUNT #92

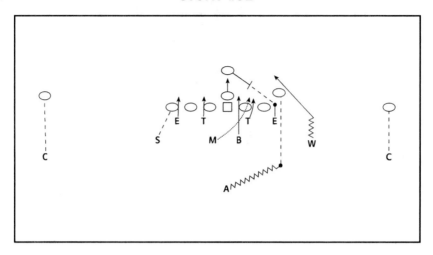

STUNT DESCRIPTION: This is a fake Assassin blitz, which incorporates a delay blitz and a weakside overload. This tactic is only possible when both #2 receivers are tight.

SECONDARY COVERAGE: A variation of zero coverage.

STUD: Covers the tight end.

STRONG END: Plays 7 technique versus run. Contains the quarterback versus pass.

STRONG TACKLE: Plays 3 technique.

MIKE: Plays base technique versus run. Versus a pass, Mike delay blitzes through the weakside B gap if ace blocks weak, and covers ace if he blocks strong.

BUCK: Blitzes through the A gap.

WEAK TACKLE: Slants into the B gap.

WEAK END: Plays 7 technique versus run. Spies ace versus pass. If ace blocks strong, the weak end continues to rush.

WHIP: Slowly creeps toward the line during cadence and rushes from the edge. Contains the quarterback and weakside run. Chases strongside run.

ASSASSIN: Covers receiver #2 weakside. Disguises his assignment by giving the quarterback a cover 1 pre-snap read.

STRONG CORNER: Covers receiver #1 (inside technique).

WEAK CORNER: Covers receiver #1 (inside technique).

STUNT #93

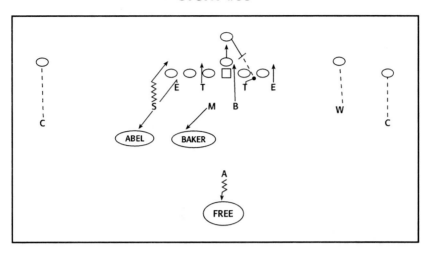

STUNT DESCRIPTION: This stunt gives the *illusion* of a six-man pass rush.

SECONDARY COVERAGE: Cover 1. Mike and the strong end drop into gumbo coverage and the weak tackle spies ace.

STUD: Creeps toward the line during cadence and rushes from the edge. Contains the quarterback and strongside run. Chases weakside run.

STRONG END: Plays 7 technique versus run. Drops Abel gumbo versus pass.

STRONG TACKLE: Plays 3 technique.

MIKE: Plays base technique versus run. Drops Baker gumbo versus pass.

BUCK: Blitzes through the A gap.

WEAK TACKLE: Plays 3 technique versus run. Spies ace if he blocks weak and continues to rush the quarterback if ace blocks strong.

WEAK END: Plays 7 technique versus run. Contains the quarterback versus pass.

WHIP: Covers receiver #2 (inside technique–lower level).

ASSASSIN: Provides alley support versus run. Plays centerfield versus pass.

STRONG CORNER: Covers receiver #1 (inside technique).

WEAK CORNER: Covers receiver #1 (inside technique–upper level).

STUNT #94

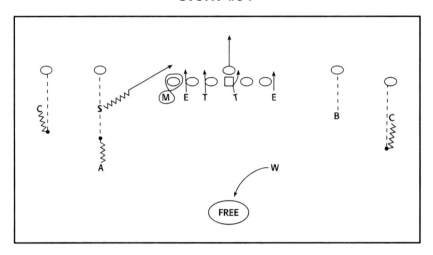

STUNT DESCRIPTION: This stunt gives the defense a five-man pass rush versus an empty formation.

SECONDARY COVERAGE: Cover 1 disguised as cover 2.

STUD: Lines up as though he's covering receiver #2 strong. Creeps inside during cadence and rushes from the edge. Contains the quarterback and strongside run. Chases weakside run.

STRONG END: Plays 5 technique.

STRONG TACKLE: Plays 3 technique.

MIKE: Plays 9 technique versus run. Covers the tight end versus pass. Jams him and funnels him inside.

BUCK: Covers receiver #2 weak (inside technique – lower level).

WEAK TACKLE: Plays 0 technique (tilt weak).

WEAK END: Plays 7 technique versus run. Contains the quarterback versus pass.

WHIP: Plays centerfield versus pass.

ASSASSIN: Lines up as though he's playing cover 2 and covers the #2 strongside receiver (inside technique–upper level).

STRONG CORNER: Covers receiver #1 (inside technique–lower level). Disguises his assignment as cover 2.

WEAK CORNER: Covers receiver #1 (inside technique–upper level). Disguises his assignment as cover 2.

STUNT #95

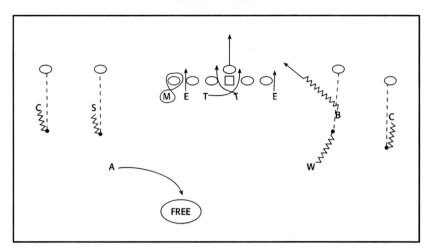

STUNT DESCRIPTION: This stunt gives the defense a five-man pass rush versus an empty formation.

SECONDARY COVERAGE: Cover 1 disguised as cover 2.

STUD: Covers #2 strongside receiver (inside technique - lower level).

STRONG END: Plays 5 technique versus run. Contains the quarterback versus pass.

STRONG TACKLE: Lines up in a 3 technique and loops behind the weak tackle into the weakside A gap.

MIKE: Plays 9 technique versus run. Covers the tight end versus pass (jam technique).

BUCK: Lines up as though he's covering receiver #2. Creeps inside during cadence and rushes from the edge. Contains the quarterback and weakside run. Chases strongside run.

WEAK TACKLE: Lines up in a 0 technique (tilt weak) and slants into the strongside A gap.

WEAK END: Plays 7 technique versus run. Contains the quarterback versus pass.

WHIP: Lines up as though he's playing cover 2. Covers the #2 weakside receiver (inside technique–lower level).

ASSASSIN: Lines up as though he's playing cover 2. Drops to centerfield at the snap.

STRONG CORNER: Covers receiver #1 (inside technique–upper level). Disguises his assignment as cover 2.

WEAK CORNER: Covers receiver #1 (inside technique–upper level). Disguises his assignment as cover 2.

STUNT #96

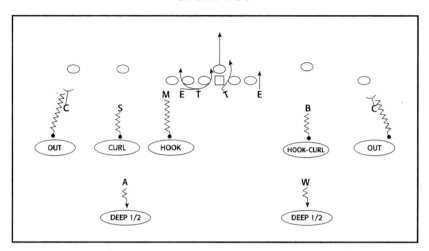

STUNT DESCRIPTION: This stunt provides the defense with a line twist and a four-man pass rush.

SECONDARY COVERAGE: Five-under, two-deep zone.

STUD: Lines up versus #2 strongside receiver and drops *curl* versus pass.

STRONG END: Lines up in a 5 technique and loops behind the tackle into the strongside A gap.

STRONG TACKLE: Lines up in a 3 technique and slants across the offensive tackle's face into the C gap. Contains the quarterback versus pass.

MIKE: Plays 9 technique versus run. Drops *hook* versus pass.

BUCK: Lines up opposite #2 weakside receiver and drops *hook-curl* versus pass.

WEAK TACKLE: Lines up in a 0 technique (tilt weak) and slants into the A gap.

WEAK END: Plays 7 technique versus run. Contains the quarterback versus pass.

WHIP: Plays deep-half coverage.

ASSASSIN: Plays deep-half coverage.

STRONG CORNER: Jams receiver #1 inside and sinks to the *out* zone.

WEAK CORNER: Jams receiver #1 inside and sinks to the *out* zone.

STUNT #97

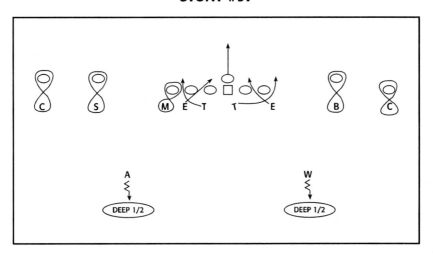

STUNT DESCRIPTION: This stunt provides the defense with a double line twist.

SECONDARY COVERAGE: Cover 2 man.

STUD: Covers #2 strongside receiver (inside trail technique).

STRONG END: Lines up in a 5 technique and slants into the B gap.

STRONG TACKLE: Lines up in a 3 technique and loops through the outside shoulder of the offensive tackle. Contains the quarterback.

MIKE: Lines up in a 9 technique and covers the tight end (outside jam technique).

BUCK: Covers #2 weakside receiver (inside trail technique).

WEAK TACKLE: Lines up in a 0 technique (tilt weak) and loops through the outside shoulder of the offensive tackle. Contains the quarterback.

WEAK END: Lines up in a 7 technique and slants through the B gap.

WHIP: Plays deep-half coverage.

ASSASSIN: Plays deep-half coverage.

STRONG CORNER: Covers receiver #1 (inside trail technique).

WEAK CORNER: Covers receiver #1 (inside trail technique).

STUNT #98

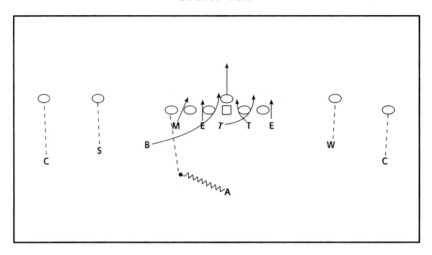

STUNT DESCRIPTION: This stunt provides the defense with a six-man pass rush.

SECONDARY COVERAGE: Zero coverage disguised as cover 1.

STUD: Covers #2 strongside receiver (inside technique-lower level).

STRONG END: Plays 3 technique.

STRONG TACKLE: Lines up in a 0 technique (tilt strong) and loops through the outside shoulder of the offensive guard into the weakside B gap.

MIKE: Lines up in a 7 technique and rushes through the C gap. Contains the quarterback.

BUCK: Lines up in an 8 technique and blitzes through the strongside A gap.

WEAK TACKLE: Lines up in a 3 technique and slants into the A gap.

WEAK END: Lines up in a 7 technique and contains the quarterback.

WHIP: Covers #2 weakside receiver (inside technique-lower level).

ASSASSIN: Lines up as though he's playing cover 1 and creeps to a position that enables him to cover the tight end.

STRONG CORNER: Covers receiver #1 (inside technique-upper level).

WEAK CORNER: Covers receiver #1 (inside technique-upper level).

STUNT #99

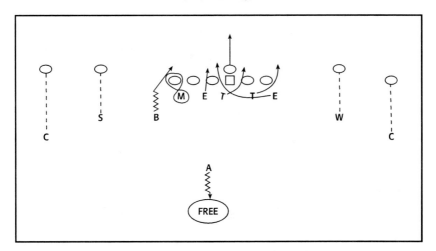

STUNT DESCRIPTION: This stunt provides the defense with a five-man pass rush.

SECONDARY COVERAGE: Cover 1.

STUD: Covers #2 strongside receiver (inside technique-lower level).

STRONG END: Plays 3 technique.

STRONG TACKLE: Lines up in a 0 technique (tilt strong) and slants into the weakside A gap.

MIKE: Lines up in a 7 technique and covers the tight end (inside trail technique).

BUCK: Lines up in an 8 technique and creeps toward the line during cadence. Rushes from the edge and contains the quarterback.

WEAK TACKLE: Lines up in a 3 technique and slants across the face of the offensive tackle into the C gap. Contains the quarterback.

WEAK END: Lines up in a 7 technique and loops into the strongside A gap.

WHIP: Covers #2 weakside receiver (inside technique-lower level).

ASSASSIN: Free, plays centerfield.

STRONG CORNER: Covers receiver #1 (inside /outside technique is dependent upon field position and the distance of #1's split).

WEAK CORNER: Covers receiver #1 (inside /outside technique is dependent upon field position and the distance of #1's split).

STUNT #100

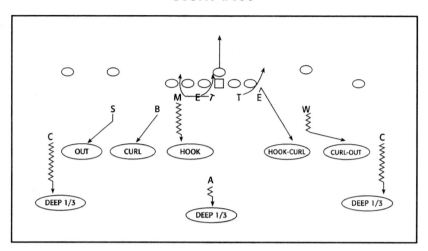

STUNT DESCRIPTION: This stunt provides the defense with a three-man pass rush, but enables it to drop eight defenders into coverage.

SECONDARY COVERAGE: Five-under, three-deep zone.

STUD: Lines up opposite #2 strongside receiver and drops into the *out* zone after denying the #2 receiver the quick seam.

STRONG END: Lines up in a 3 technique and slants into the A gap.

STRONG TACKLE: Lines up in a 0 technique (tilt strong) and slants across the tackle's face into the strongside C gap. Contains the quarterback.

MIKE: Lines up in a 7 technique and drops *hook* versus pass.

BUCK: Lines up in an 8 technique and drops *curl* versus pass.

WEAK TACKLE: Lines up in a 3 technique and slants across the face of the offensive tackle into the C gap. Contains the quarterback.

WEAK END: Lines up in a 7 technique and drops *hook-curl* versus pass.

WHIP: Lines up inside of the #2 weakside receiver and drops *curl-out* versus pass.

ASSASSIN: Plays deep middle-third coverage.

STRONG CORNER: Plays deep outside-third coverage.

WEAK CORNER: Plays deep outside-third coverage.

STUNT #101

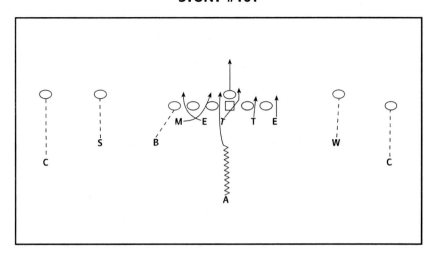

STUNT DESCRIPTION: This stunt provides the defense with a six-man pass rush and an Assassin blitz.

SECONDARY COVERAGE: Zero coverage disguised as cover 1.

STUD: Covers #2 strongside receiver (inside technique-lower level).

STRONG END: Lines up in a 3 technique and slants across the offensive tackle's face into the C gap. Contains the quarterback.

STRONG TACKLE: Lines up in a 0 (tilt strong) technique and slants into the weakside A gap.

MIKE: Lines up in a 7 technique and loops behind the end into the B gap.

BUCK: Lines up in an 8 technique and covers the tight end.

WEAK TACKLE: Plays a 3 technique.

WEAK END: Lines up in a 7 technique and contains the quarterback.

WHIP: Covers #2 weakside receiver (inside technique-lower level).

ASSASSIN: Lines up as though he's playing cover 1. Creeps toward the line during cadence and blitzes through the strongside A gap.

STRONG CORNER: Covers receiver #1 (inside technique-upper level).

WEAK CORNER: Covers receiver #1 (inside technique-upper level).

About the Author

Leo Hand assumed the position of the defensive backfield coach at Andress High School in 2004. In Hand's first season as secondary coach at Andress, the team had an 11-1 record and won a bi-district championship. They allowed opponents an average of only 7.7 points per game, had 20 interceptions, and allowed only three touchdown passes to be scored against them during the entire 2004 season.

Hand previously served as the defensive coordinator at El Paso (Texas) High School from 2001 to 2003. Prior to that, he held the same position with Irvin High School in El Paso, Texas. With over 36 years of experience as a teacher and coach, Hand has served in a variety of coaching positions in his career—achieving a notable level of success at each stop.

A graduate of Emporia State University in Emporia, Kansas, Hand began his football-coaching career in 1968 as the junior varsity coach for McQuaid Jesuit High School in Rochester, New York. After two seasons, Hand accepted the job as the offensive line coach at Aquinas Institute (1970 -1971), and then served as the head coach at Saint John Fisher College for two years. Hand has also served on the gridiron staffs at APW (Parrish, NY) High School (head coach); Saint Anthony (Long Beach, CA) High School (head coach); Daniel Murphy (Los Angeles, CA) High School (head coach); Servite (Anaheim, CA) High School (head coach); Serra (Gardena, CA) High School (head coach); Long Beach (CA) City College (offensive line and linebackers); and Los Angeles (CA) Harbor College (offensive coordinator).

During the last six years that he spent coaching interscholastic teams in California, Hand's squads won 81 percent of their games in the highly competitive area of Southern California. At Serra High School, his teams compiled a 24-1 record, won a CIF championship, and were declared California state champions. Hand has helped rebuild several floundering gridiron teams into highly successful programs. Hand has been honored on numerous occasions with Coach of the Year recognition for his efforts.

A former Golden Gloves boxing champion, Hand is a prolific author. He has written several football instructional books and published numerous articles. With his wife, Mary, Hand has nine children and 11 grandchildren.